THE COTTAGE ON MYSTIC LANE

THE SAINTS OF SAVANNAH SERIES

LEIGH EBBERWEIN

Old Fort Press
Savannah, Georgia

The Cottage on Mystic Lane
Copyright © 2024 by Leigh Ebberwein
Library of Congress Control Number: 2024907532

All rights reserved. Published in the United States by Old Fort Press LLC, Savannah, Ga.

www.oldfortpress.com

No part of this book may be reproduced in any form or by any electronic or mechanical means, including information storage and retrieval systems, without written permission from the author, except for the use of brief quotations in a book review.
This book is a work of fiction. Names, characters, places, and events either are the product of the author's imagination or used fictitiously. Any resemblance to persons, living or dead, is entirely coincidental.

ISBN: 978-1-7376152-9-3 (Paperback)
ISBN: 978-1-964278-00-1 (E-book)

CONTENTS

1. Lottie	1
2. Embracing Change	5
3. Family	9
4. Order	15
5. General Oglethorpe Hotel	19
6. The Letter	22
7. Coincidence	26
8. A Call Home	30
9. The Dance	33
10. The Crystal	39
11. Gladys	43
12. Turner Creek	48
13. Wedding Bells	53
14. The Chapel	57
15. Savannah Archives	62
16. Oystering	67
17. The Oyster Stew Crew	72
18. Uncle Carl	77
19. Youth Group	82
20. Guatemala	86
21. The Shed	91
22. The Mystic	96
23. Stairs of Death	102
24. Introductions	108
25. Just You, Me and the Sea	112
26. Goodbye, Gladys	117
27. God Wink	122
28. Comparing Stews	127
29. All Saints Day	132
30. When the Lights Go Out	138
31. Welcome to Prince Edward Island	144
32. One-Half	149
33. Cavendish	154

34. Farm to Table	161
35. This is My Island	166
36. Matching Birthdays	171
37. Off to Sea	176
38. Coming Home	181
39. Making their Rounds	185
40. The Family Bloodline	189
41. Snowed In	195
42. Darkness and Light	201
43. The Plan	207
44. Homebound	212
45. Goodbye Letters	217
46. The Spirit World	222
47. Thorns	227
48. Manly	231
49. Filtering Water	236
50. Au Revoir	241
51. Southern Charm	245
52. Treasure	250
53. Free	256
54. Protectors	259
Also by Leigh Ebberwein	267
Acknowledgments	271
Epilogue	273
STOP BY FOR A VISIT	279

1

LOTTIE

Four Years Prior

Moonlight seeped through the branches of the mysterious oaks in Bonaventure Cemetery, making the headstones appear to glow. The outdoor smell of dirt and rot was always present. Its proximity to the Wilmington River heightened the scent, especially on a low tide. Agnes breathed in deeply, allowing the smell of the marsh to tickle her nose. Savannahians were like that; they embraced the acrid scent. Some, like Agnes, even longed for it.

She let her eyes dance around the Victorian cemetery. How had she allowed this to continue? But when she focused on her beloved Aunt Lottie, she knew the reason. It had become their tradition. She felt a lump forming in her throat as she pictured Lottie alone in the cemetery the following year. Lost in her thoughts, she hadn't noticed Lottie's approach until a wave of Chanel No. 5 passed. Turning, she watched Lottie move toward the tombstones and prepared herself for the stories detailing each one.

"These are your great-grandparents," Lottie began, pointing

to the headstones directly at their feet. Agnes knew the speech well. She had been in the cemetery with Lottie since she was a small child. Lottie always felt the need to introduce the people who lay beneath. "They died in the late 1940s and early 1950s. These are my sisters; there were three of us: me, Lizzie, and Gladys. Lizzie, your grandmother, as you know, just passed two years ago." Lottie paused and made the Sign of the Cross before continuing to the next headstone. "Gladys went missing in 1938, so they put 1938 on her tombstone. But remember, Agnes, she went missing. The casket is empty. And finally, this is my beloved husband, Benjamin. He died three months after your birthday. I remember holding you at his funeral."

"I'm sorry I never met him," Agnes added.

"Oh, but you did, Agnes. You did." Agnes looked at her curiously.

"Right. Well, I'm sorry I don't remember him."

Lottie nodded her head and belted out an order. "Now, light the candles, Agnes. It's almost time."

Agnes lit the long taper candles in the candelabra on the beautifully dressed card table. Aunt Lottie had the process down to a tee. She would bring hors d'oeuvres and mix a batch of martinis, just like they did more than fifty years ago when her husband asked for her hand in marriage.

Agnes was always confused by the fact that her aunt continued to celebrate—and count—wedding anniversaries after her husband passed away twenty-two years ago. "Tell me again, how many years you were married?" Agnes asked.

"This is a big one. We're celebrating our fiftieth anniversary." Her aunt knew what she was thinking and explained, "You're still married even though they are in another room."

Or, in a tiny room six feet under the ground of this creepy cemetery, Agnes thought to herself.

"I heard that," her aunt said, and Agnes knew she had. Even if it had not been said out loud.

Her aunt had always been able to read Agnes' mind. When she was a little girl, Aunt Lottie knew all her secrets. As Agnes grew older, she learned tricks to keep her thoughts guarded. But occasionally, when Agnes felt vulnerable, her defenses flew out the window. "I'm sorry, Aunt Lottie, but you know I feel differently about cemeteries than you."

Aunt Lottie smiled widely, showing off her perfectly straight bridge of false teeth. "I hope you'll soon embrace your gifts too, my dear."

Their eyes met, showing their affection for one another in a brief glance, but they were interrupted when the mantle clock Lottie had brought began its nine chimes. Lottie hurriedly handed Agnes a martini glass. Holding it up in a toast, she began.

"Just like you told me fifty years ago today, Benjamin. Our love is eternal, now and forever. Although I miss seeing your face, I still treasure our conversations. I can't wait to be with you once again. But until then, you still and always will have my heart. Cheers, my love, and cheers to our sweet niece, Aggie. May she find a love like ours."

The glasses clinking sounded like an explosion. Agnes worriedly looked at Aunt Lottie while she ran her finger around the rim of the glass, hoping not to nick it on a crack. "We better be careful out here. That loud sound might stir up the ghost of Gracie."

"Ah, Gracie isn't here. That little girl's spirit is still playing in the streets on Barnard, in front of the old Pulaski House."

"How do you know all this?" Agnes asked with a timid smile.

Lottie answered, "She's just in the next room." Winking, she finished the conversation and reached for a canapé on the silver tray.

Agnes followed, grabbing a mini crab cake and popping it in her mouth. The taste of butter crackers and capers enhanced the flavor of the lump crab meat. "Yum! I always love it when you put the crab cakes on the brunch menu at Lottie's, but the ones tonight might just be your best batch yet."

"They always taste better on a full moon. Our tastebuds are more alive," Lottie explained as she looked down at the graves she had visited for eighteen years with Agnes.

"I'm gonna miss being out here with you when I'm at college next year," Agnes admitted. She felt the lump rise in her throat again, knowing how hard it would be to leave Lottie behind.

"Who knows? You might be able to come home at that time," Lottie replied. Agnes narrowed her eyes as Lottie shrugged, adding, "You never know."

That statement made Agnes laugh. "I never know, but you always know."

"Not everything," Lottie answered, letting her gaze fall onto her husband's tombstone before returning to Agnes. "I sure am gonna miss you next year. I love you like my own." She pulled Agnes in for a peck on her cheek, but her aunt's eyes quickly darted toward the Intercoastal Waterway. "Now, drink up. We need to finish these martinis before the fog sets in. You never want to be in the cemetery when there's fog."

They finished the hors d'oeuvres and cocktails and began to load the car. As soon as they climbed in and started the vehicle, the fog began to roll in. Agnes watched as it moved toward them like a blanket being pulled over a sleeping child. As the mist passed each grave, it grew thicker.

"Buckle up and hold on," Lottie commanded as she stepped on the gas, pulling out of the dirt lane of plot three. The fog reached its fingers toward the car's bumper as it pulled out the main gate to safety. Only then did she ease up on the gas pedal as the 1965 Saab puttered around the winding curves of Bonaventure Road.

2

EMBRACING CHANGE

Agnes settled on the snow-covered kneeler, unsure how she had even gotten there. While walking home from practice, she was pulled in another direction. Her brain could not comprehend the longing in her heart, but she knew she needed help. She could no longer continue down the path she had chosen for herself a year ago when she decided to attend Notre Dame. Looking back, she wondered if she had actually chosen it for herself at all, or did it choose her?

Agnes shivered involuntarily. When would she ever become accustomed to the bitter cold of South Bend, Indiana? Everyone told her that she had thin, Southern blood that would eventually thicken, but she wasn't sure she could wait much longer. She was miserable and only wanted to be home in Savannah.

Her eyes focused on the many lit candles inside the belly of the Grotto. So many prayer intentions burning through the night. Somehow, the thought of the people who had lit them gave her the strength to pinpoint her prayer. She closed her eyes and whispered, "I can't keep up with my classes. I can't keep up with the team, and I'm so cold I can't think. Why? Why am I here?" Opening her eyes, she let them wander up the Grotto's stone front to focus on the statue of Mary, illuminated by spotlights. She felt the lump grow in her throat. "Dear Mary, please intercede on my behalf to your Son to send me a sign on how to continue."

Closing her eyes again, she felt the tears moving down her cheeks and prayed they wouldn't turn to ice. She was surprised when she felt the kneeler shift, throwing her off balance. She thrust out her hands to grasp the rail but couldn't quite reach it. As she began to fall, the person responsible for her imbalance grabbed her in a bear hug.

Agnes sighed with relief, briefly enjoying the human interaction before looking into Matthew Monroe's face. She quickly pushed him away and stood. Glaring at the statue, she mumbled, "Matthew? Really?"

"I've been looking everywhere for you. Do you come here often?" he teased while wagging his eyebrows.

She glanced at him sideways. "As a matter of fact, I do. Almost every night."

"Yeah, I come here daily, too, but usually in the morning before classes."

She nodded, holding him a little higher in regard but still aggravated with him. "Why were you looking for me, Matt? My brothers send you? Or Jack?"

"Maybe. Or maybe I wanted to check on you myself." She gave him a knowing look until he told the truth. "Okay. Your brothers were worried about you after Christmas break, so I told them I would look in on you. Seriously, how are you doing?"

His face showed genuine concern. Besides, she asked for help, and he showed up, so she should give him a chance.

"It sure ain't Savannah," she said in a whisper.

"I know. Isn't it great?"

Agnes burst out crying, leaving Matthew confused about how to handle the emotional train wreck standing in front of him. He awkwardly began to pat her back until she turned into his arms, crying on his shoulder. He slowly wrapped his arms around her until they hugged her tightly.

"It will get better, Agnes," he whispered into her hair, holding her until her tears slowed. As much as he didn't want to let her go, he pulled back to see her face. Speaking softly, he said, "I promise it will get better. You must embrace the change and stop trying to keep one foot in Savannah. Make South Bend your home. Get involved. Get a job. Go on the summer mission trips Notre Dame puts on. Then, after four years, if you choose, move home. But you'll always have this amazing college experience under your belt."

He wiped her wet cheeks with his gloved hand. "I struggled at first, too. But now that I'm in my last year, time is flying." He paused, then continued, "But you won't catch me back in Savannah. I've enjoyed being so close to Chicago. Hopefully, I'll get an offer this year or next, and I can move."

He realized he had been talking too long and looked down at Agnes. She was cute, all bundled up in her puffy jacket with the candlelight from the many prayer intentions twinkling in her deep brown eyes. He felt the electricity between them again, but he had to keep it at bay and stay focused. Bending down, he locked eyes with her. "You've got this. Get involved. Commit to living here. You'll be..." His words trailed off when he noticed her lips quivering from crying. He could no longer keep his distance. Leaning over, he kissed her softly on the lips.

Her eyes flew open when they parted. *WHAT WAS THAT?* she asked herself, as laughter began to erupt from deep inside her. She had never experienced a feeling like that before, and instantly, all her problems disappeared. But her exhilaration was quickly squashed by the look on Matthew's face. The only word to describe it was fear.

"Goodbye, Agnes," was all he said as he left her.

She tried her best not to watch him as he walked away, but she couldn't help herself. She was happy when he paused before walking up the stairs. But once he was out of sight, he was out of her life—at least for the time being.

3

FAMILY

Present Day

Agnes smiled as she listened to the happy sounds of her family through the kitchen door. Stepping inside, she was hit by the savory smell of beef and gravy. Everyone at the table welcomed her, each in their own unique way. Some teased, and others reprimanded her for being late, but each comment was made with love.

She stood motionless. Her last spring break was coming to an end, and she didn't know when she would be back home. She wanted to remember this moment, so she watched her family intently. Her pause must have alarmed her mother, who flew to her feet and walked toward Agnes. "I made your favorite," she said, straightening Agnes' hair with her hand and tucking a runaway piece behind her ear.

Agnes took an exaggerated smell and smiled. "Pot roast. Thanks, Mom."

Her dad and brothers began to tease her. "The only time we get Mom's pot roast is when you come home."

Her mom hushed them and instructed Agnes to wash up and fix her plate.

Her seat at the six-person table was open. The same seat she had sat in her entire life. But somehow, it now appeared very narrow—probably due to her now adult brothers, Chris and Bobby, sitting on either side. She wondered if her seat sat open for the last four years, giving her brothers room to spread out. Turning to each, she asked, "What are you guys doing here?"

"We're here almost every night, sis. We're growing boys," her brother Chris answered, his blue eyes twinkling as he flexed his bicep muscle in her direction.

"You're twenty-eight years old, Chris. The only direction you're still growing is out, not up," she teased, motioning her hands around her belly. She then turned to Bobby. "You don't even live here anymore, and I heard Katie is a great cook."

"She is, but it's girls' night out," Bobby answered. His eyes grazed over Agnes' head and locked with Chris'. They nodded to each other and scooted their chairs toward Agnes, boxing her in.

"Oh no, you don't," she yelled.

Her brothers threw their hands in the air and began to bump around in their chairs, pretending to be on a roller coaster ride like they had done so many times before. "Get ready, Agnes. We're almost at the top, and it's gonna be a bumpy ride," they cried out.

"I'm not playing. Come on, guys. I'm hungry," Agnes begged.

Her dad jumped up and pulled her full plate of pot roast to safety just before the roller coaster began its downward zoom. The roller coaster traveled left, right, up, and down while her brothers poked and tickled Agnes. By the time the pretend car finally pulled back into the station, Agnes and the rest of the table were laughing hysterically.

"I sure missed you guys," she told them, kissing each one on the cheek.

"We miss you, too, Aggie," Chris answered.

"All right, boys. Let Agnes enjoy her favorite meal," her mom reprimanded, and everyone settled in.

Agnes locked eyes with her brother Tim, who still shook his head at the situation. "Wanna trade seats?" he asked sympathetically.

"Not a chance," Agnes answered with a sideways grin, rubbing the poke marks on her side. It had always been like that; her brothers treated her like one of them, pulling her along on their many adventures. They had encouraged her to play basketball, but they were never easy on her; they made her into the athlete she was. Sometimes, she wondered if she should thank them or condemn them.

Her mom interrupted her thoughts. "I just wanted to let you know I'm not spoiling your brothers. It's just hard to cook for two, so I invite the boys over whenever I cook."

Agnes hadn't noticed that her mom had become quiet when she had questioned her brothers, but she realized she had hit a nerve, although she wasn't sure which one. "I think it's great, Mom. And if I were home, I'd be here every night. No one can beat your cooking," she answered, watching the relief move across her mom's face.

Her dad chimed in. "We love it when our kids are around." Then, with a mischievous grin, he winked at his wife and added, "And we like our time alone, too. Don't we, Ruthie?"

The table erupted with "Ewws," making her dad chuckle.

Agnes shook her head and smiled, remembering how crazy it always was around the dinner table. The boys shoveled gross amounts of food into their mouths while knocking each other around. Her parents no doubt appreciated their empty nest, so she didn't feel guilty about moving to Chicago after graduation.

"How was your visit to Bonaventure with Lottie this year?" her dad asked.

"Exactly the same as every year," Agnes answered with a sly smile. "I hate that I won't be here for her next year. I doubt they'll let me off of work."

"That's what you said the year you went to Notre Dame, and somehow your spring breaks have lined up with her wedding anniversary," her mom answered.

"Somehow," she whispered, nodding to her mom with acknowledgment.

"Lottie came by when we were having dinner a few weeks ago," Bobby announced, his red hair bouncing around as he talked. "She got on to us for talking with our mouths full. She said, 'Silence is golden,' to make us stop talking, then began telling us the story about the missing treasure from the Civil War. Whenever she finds us all together, she retells the story. Sometimes, I actually believe it exists. I swear, the story gets better and better."

"I agree, or maybe now we could use $100,000 in gold coins," Tim added.

Agnes egged them on. "Remind me how the story goes."

"She told us there are three graves in the Savannah area that lay side by side. They are gravestones with a colonel's name on each, and the gold was buried in the only one who was actually a colonel in the Confederacy. The other two were decoys."

"But why would someone bury gold and leave it?"

"They intended to come back and get it to try and win the Civil War, but they never got a chance," Bobby explained, then ran his fingers across his throat, signaling the infamous colonel had died.

"So, the money is just sitting there, waiting for you?" Agnes teased. When they all nodded their heads in excitement, she burst their bubble. "But where?"

Her mom intervened. "I can tell you that it's not in any cemetery in Savannah. I've taken you to every one of them multiple times. We've walked and walked, searching for the names of colonels. People have been looking for years. Every once in a while, you'll hear it come back up in the news, but the gold has never been found."

"It doesn't exist," Agnes spit out with a pretend cough.

Bobby poked her in the side. "Oh yes, it does, and Lottie made us promise to split it evenly between all of us when we find it."

"Now you're talking. Treasure split four ways. When can we go back to the cemeteries?" she teased.

Bobby looked at her questioningly. "You're just messing with me, aren't you?" She first shrugged her shoulders and then began to nod. He poked harder until she yelped, then added, "You'll see. We're gonna find it one of these days."

Agnes softened and nudged him with her elbow. "I can't wait," she whispered and was happy when he gave her a small smile.

Agnes finally dove into her favorite meal, enjoying the melt-in-your-mouth beef, carrots, and baby red potatoes all mixed perfectly in a brown gravy poured over white rice. On the side were green beans and biscuits. She set her biscuit on a separate plate, and once she finished everything else, she pulled the Mrs. Butterworth syrup from the pantry and poured it on her plate. She dipped each piece, carefully covering each bite in sweetness. "I had a great time at the half-rubber tournament yesterday," Agnes announced, picturing the throngs of people who lined Tybee the day before. Spring break reassured all of Savannah that summer was not far away, and the annual half-rubber game brought the whole community together.

Most people would come later in the day to watch the final game, but young women, college and high school alike, were drawn to the bare-chested, athletic young men battling it out on the beach.

"Those Harrigans," Tim said with a growl.

"I'm so sorry about last night's game. I really thought you guys had them," Agnes commented.

"We would have, too, if the tide hadn't come in so high," Chris added.

Bobby shook his head, "We didn't even think to check and see if there was a king tide. And isn't it just our luck that it came in so fast in the last inning? We were ahead. If only they hadn't been last at-bat. That freezing water put our left fielder in the ocean past his knees. He just couldn't get to that fly ball."

"If nothing else, this year will go down in history," Chris added. "It's the year the tide stole the championship half-rubber ball."

4

ORDER

"Order," Lottie muttered out loud, pondering what lay ahead. "Things must be in order." Slowly, she ran her eyes around the room. This was her space, and it would soon be Agnes'. Everything must be in order.

Lottie had always cleaned her home from top to bottom before leaving for a trip, knowing it was easier to get back to normal when everything was in order. But this time, she was cleaning up her life, from top to bottom, for a one-way trip. The sound of her sigh startled her. It was filled with desperation and sadness. But in all actuality, she was neither of the two. She had lived a good life and wasn't afraid of what was next. She only worried about the person she was leaving behind and knew she must have everything in order for Agnes.

She knew her fate. She had known for quite some time. In the beginning, she had thought that knowing was a blessing. It would give her time to finish all the things she needed to. But in all her planning, she had not anticipated that each person in her plan was constantly making decisions that changed her course. As always, she surrendered all her worries to the only person who could alleviate them. "Jesus, I trust in you. You always know best." That one simple statement, straight from the heart, gave her the peace she needed. A small smile formed on her mouth as her thoughts returned to Agnes. She had arranged to see her one more time before she went back to school. One more time. No, the last time. The thought put a lump in her throat, but she swallowed it down quickly. Today, she would say her goodbyes and reassure Agnes that all would be well. Today, she would have one last meal with her favorite person on this earth.

Agnes was surprised to find the restaurant closed when she arrived and wondered if she had misunderstood where they were to meet. But the many smells of Lottie's cooking wafted through the air, inviting her inside. Agnes walked down the path on the side of the building, pausing to run her hand down a stalk of rosemary that extended from the garden, then entered through the kitchen's back door.

Lottie was standing at the stove, singing and swaying while she cooked. Agnes watched briefly before entering, trying to record the image to memory. *She's glowing,* Agnes thought. *And she looks so young.*

Lottie turned under the weight of Agnes' stare, the glow replaced by her beaming smile. She quickly closed the distance between them and wrapped Agnes in a tight hug while still holding her spatula in the air. "I'm so happy you're here. Hungry?"

"I wasn't until I smelled your cooking."

Lottie walked over to the sizzling pan and speared a large shrimp with a fork. With a mischievous grin, she held it out to Agnes. "Look here, girlie."

"You made me shrimp & grits?"

"Of course I did, my love."

Agnes looked at her sideways. "You only make that when I'm sad about something, and I'm not sad about anything right now. What's up?"

"Pooey. I make shrimp and grits because they're your favorite and always make you happy. Now grab a dish and serve us up a plate. You know how it's done."

Agnes followed directions and plated two servings of the Southern dish while Lottie made them both a cup of coffee and a plate of cheddar biscuits. As they walked to their favorite booth inside the restaurant, Agnes asked, "Why are you closed today?"

"Not just today. I'm closed for restructuring."

"Restructuring? What does that mean?"

"That means the time has come for me to retire." Lottie held her cards close to her chest, not wanting to worry Agnes.

"Are you selling Lottie's?" Agnes asked worriedly.

"Why? You wanna buy it?" Lottie patted Agnes' hand and quickly continued before Agnes could answer. "When you know, you know. And it's time for me to leave." Lottie felt Agnes watching her closely, playing out their conversation. Finally, she added, "Enough about me. Tell me about you. You're leaving tomorrow to finish the last few weeks of school. That's exciting. How was your spring break?"

Agnes began telling Lottie about the half-rubber game and school. They talked and talked, each taking turns getting up to refill their coffees.

"This is the last time I'll eat in this restaurant. I'm so happy it was with you." Lottie squeezed Agnes' hand. "Everything I have will be yours. You are the closest thing to a child I've ever known, and I am most grateful to you. You will learn many things over the next year. Some things might rock you to the very core. But know this, you are loved by many in this life and the next." She raised her hand and kissed it softly before adding, "You'll come home for my funeral, won't you?"

"Aunt Lottie, don't talk like that," Agnes chided.

Her aunt grabbed her hand tightly, requiring an answer. "Won't you?" she asked once more.

"Absolutely," Agnes answered warily. "You couldn't keep me away. But what are you not telling me?"

Lottie smiled, letting her eyes linger on Agnes' face for a long moment before announcing, "Your friends are here."

Agnes looked around the empty room curiously, then back at Lottie, who pointed out the window seconds before the tribe walked up.

"How do you do that?" Agnes asked.

"The same way you will. One day."

Lottie unlocked the door to Agnes' friends, who surrounded Lottie with a group hug. She laughed, doting on each of them. "Oh, how I love you girls. Never forget that, Okay?"

"We love you, too," they replied, quickly adding, "What's that we smell?"

That made Lottie the happiest of all. Feeding people makes every Southern cook happy, and she had been feeding Agnes' tribe for years through happy times and sad times. She knew what each of them needed. Agnes was going to need all of them in the many months ahead.

5

GENERAL OGLETHORPE HOTEL

Lottie felt the pull to a different time. That sometimes happened; the past and present would dance with one another until time almost overlapped. Her mind would focus on a place and time, and she could re-live it. Today was the last summer she and her two sisters, Gladys and Lizzie, spent together on Wilmington Island. So that afternoon, she hopped into her Saab and drove to that spot.

She walked down the long dock. The original one was long gone, swept away from the rotting of the tides and the wind from many hurricanes. Its replacement felt different. It was longer and had a benched area at the end, but the scene around it was exactly the same. Lottie looked over the marsh and was carried back to the summer of 1938.

She enjoyed working at the General Oglethorpe Hotel. It was her home away from home. Her father had managed the old hotel for as long as she could remember. He was actually their first employee, hired as it was being built.

Every summer since, she and her two sisters, Gladys and Lizzie, would move into a hotel room reserved for the staff and work for the General Oglethorpe Hotel. Their mother would come to visit quite often but would always leave before dark to cross the draw bridge back to Ardsley Park. She would tell them she must take care of their home during the summer, but the truth of the matter was that raising three teenage daughters during the school year was hard work, so she enjoyed her quiet time catching up on her reading and doing small projects around the house. "There is always something that needs to be done when you own a home," she would tell them and her home was run well. She deserved the rest.

The three sisters always loved spending their summers together around the hotel. They called themselves the Three Musketeers because they were inseparable. It helped that there were only eighteen months between each of them. But that summer felt different. She thought their closeness in age might be hammering a wedge of jealousy. If only that had been the case.

On that particular night, they were scheduled to work the July 4th party, the main event of the summer. The hotel was always fully booked, but in July, big wigs from all over the country would reserve the various villas for the month to be at the big party. People would also come from around the Savannah area, mostly by boat, to enjoy all the festivities, especially the fireworks.

The party would last all night. The guests with children would enjoy the hotel's family activities during the day, but the evening was adults only, beginning at 9 p.m. and ending with a sunrise breakfast buffet.

The staff had been instructed to pamper this small group the whole week prior. "Give them anything they want, and don't speak unless they ask you a question." That night, the most important guest of the evening wanted three bottles of champagne delivered to his enormous yacht sitting at the end of the longest slip, exclusively away from the other boats, and Lizzie had been asked to deliver it.

As she gathered the bottles into her arms, Gladys took control. "This is too much for you, Lizzie. You are the biggest klutz out of all of us, and I am the oldest. I deserve the privilege to deliver the champagne and to get the tip." Lizzie turned immediately to Lottie, who shrugged and rolled her eyes, and then she handed the bottles over to Gladys.

Lottie jolted back to the present. Taking a deep breath, she stared across the Wilmington River. *How could I not see what would happen that night?* she wondered. With a slight nod, she answered her own question. *Because life would have been different if I had stopped it.* "Still, I wonder," she whispered, letting the words fly into the saltwater breeze.

6

THE LETTER

The news of Lottie's death came the day after Agnes' graduation. The family was staying at the Morris Inn in South Bend, Indiana when the call came. They were told that Lottie had died in her sleep and was found by a friend who transported her to her weekly hair appointment every Monday.

Agnes had been with her parents when they received the news but soon realized she needed time alone. She wandered onto the hotel's stone courtyard and found a table with an open umbrella. Wiping the dew from the iron seat, she settled into the overstuffed cushion and let the news sink in. It had only been a few weeks since Aunt Lottie had asked if Agnes would come home for her funeral. The thought of them sitting at Lottie's, eating shrimp and grits, made her smile. *I wonder if she knew when we were together?* Agnes knew the answer as soon as the thought popped into her head. *Lottie waited until after I finished school, but before I laid roots in Chicago.* A gentle breeze rattled the umbrella, and Agnes swore she smelled Chanel No. 5. *Surely, I'm imagining that.* She closed her eyes to smell once again.

The sound of her mother's voice pulled her back to reality. "Agnes, are you okay, sweetheart?"

Agnes smiled as her mother sat in the chair beside her. "I will be, Mom."

Her mother nodded in acknowledgment. "I know you must be at your new job on Wednesday. I'm sure Aunt Lottie would have understood."

Agnes laughed, which was not the response her mother was expecting. Clearing her throat, Agnes answered. "Thanks, Mom, but Chicago can wait." Her mother opened her mouth to challenge her, but Agnes only shook her head. "It'll keep, Mom," she whispered, but she knew deep in her heart that Chicago would now wait indefinitely.

"No!" Gladys screamed into her quiet house, then read through the letter again, hoping she had misunderstood its contents. Her eyes blurred from tears, but she wiped them as they fell until she saw her sister's signature at the end.

>Gladys,
>
>Tomorrow will be my last day in this world. I leave with the satisfaction of knowing we succeeded in keeping you safe over the last fifty years. However, if this story isn't told, your secret dies with me, and that's not fair to Agnes. I believe it's time for you to come home and meet her. She deserves to know the truth.
>
>There has been nothing suspicious since you last visited Savannah. Although the jewels are still missing, they will be discovered much later.
>
>I've enclosed a plane ticket that will take you to Savannah for my funeral. And Gladys, if you ever wondered—I know!
>
>Your sister, Lottie

Lottie had always been in touch with the spiritual world, so the fact that she was aware of the date of her own passing didn't shock Gladys. Still, the fact she sent a plane ticket meant she had no doubts. Gladys' hands trembled as she moved to the part that most upset her. "She knows," she whispered. The weight of those two words physically hurt. She placed her hand over the pain stabbing in her stomach. Her sister knew what she had done. She had always wondered. With Lottie's gifts, she could have known the moment it happened. But surely, she would have confronted Gladys long before now.

Gladys pulled the letter to her chest and let her mind travel back to the day Lottie had been born. She was barely three years old, but she would never forget it. It had been her mother's third delivery, and Lottie came so quickly that they didn't have time to make it to the hospital. Gladys had been toweling the floor when the doctor arrived, and Lottie was born just minutes afterward. The room had been loud with the screams of childbirth but went completely quiet. The silence confused Gladys, so she walked to her mother's bedside to witness the doctor cutting through the veil that covered the baby's face.

From that day forward, their mother treated Lottie differently. Lottie argued that it was because she was the baby of the three girls, but Gladys knew it was because she had been an encaul birth. Babies born with the amniotic sac still across their faces were an anomaly and were known to have spiritual gifts. This held true in Lottie.

Gladys saw those gifts come to fruition. Although their family were strong Catholics, Lottie had a connection and understanding of her faith that others spent a lifetime trying to obtain. Their whole family was confident she would join religious life in one shape or another, but Lottie was happy in Savannah. She loved to cook, and her dishes brought joy and comfort to anyone who ate them. It was no surprise when she opened a restaurant.

Over the years, Lottie became extremely close to Agnes. So, when Lottie noticed similar gifts in her niece, she completely let down her guard and began to share her abilities and her thoughts about how to use them in a faith-filled way. In one of her many letters, Lottie told Gladys, "We are kindred spirits. But she needs to know the truth."

Now, once again, she was asking Gladys to tell the truth. "The truth?" Gladys whispered. "I barely remember the truth these days." She pushed herself up, struggling to stand. Slowly, she made her way to the door and walked onto the large porch. The view of Charlottetown from her deck always comforted her, but nothing could ease her worries today. Pulling her sweater higher on her neck, she breathed in the salt air from the harbor.

"Agnes," she whispered into the wind. Her thoughts immediately jumped to Henri, and her throat tightened in response. "Breathe," she told herself when she realized she was holding her breath. In through the nose and out through the mouth. But no amount of breathing could erase the picture of standing at his graveside from her mind. Then the guilt hit. *When was the last time I visited his grave?* she wondered. *I haven't been to Cavendish in months.* So many memories. So many secrets.

She had been lost in her thoughts. She didn't realize the sun had set until the spotlights on the cathedral began to glow. "I owe it to Henri to meet his daughter. She deserves to know the truth," she muttered, adding, "But no one will ever know the whole truth."

7

COINCIDENCE

Lottie's funeral was unique, just like Lottie herself. She had planned it to the mark and left no room for questions. Agnes had been asked to give a eulogy after the graveside service and had been given an envelope the day prior that read, "My Eulogy."

When the funeral was over, Agnes began reading as instructed. But halfway in, she noticed that the circumstances around her began to coincide with what she was reading.

"Just like the ships going out to sea, we are not meant to stay in this port forever."

Agnes, pause here for the ship's whistle.

Agnes wasn't surprised to hear the long blow in the distance. Everyone laughed at the coincidence, but only Agnes knew how her speech read. She continued reading until she got to the end.

"And finally, we want to thank those who made a long trip home for the funeral."

Agnes, pause here and make eye contact with the lady standing beside my sister, Gladys' empty grave.

When Agnes did as the letter said, she was surprised to see the older lady nod.

She knows, thought Agnes. *But how does she know? And who is she?*

As she finished her Eulogy, Agnes was swamped by people offering their condolences. For the next several minutes, she visited with her family and walked with her friends to their car. The tribe was close to Lottie and was saddened by her passing until Agnes showed them a copy of her Eulogy.

"Oh my gosh, Agnes. She knew what would happen at her own funeral," Maggie remarked.

"As creepy as that is, I'm not surprised," Latrice added.

Agnes jumped in quickly, "I'm really not either. But the first time I read it, I doubted it. Then, when it all fell into place, I was stunned. I mean, come on. She knew when a ship would blow its whistle?"

"Ships blow their whistles all the time. Maybe it really was a coincidence," Jan said.

Agnes shook her head. "Lottie always told me there's no such thing as coincidences."

"And she would know," Stephanie agreed. She leaned closer and asked, "I didn't want to ask before, but where is Bradley? Is everything okay?"

Agnes was surprised that the mention of Bradley's name hadn't upset her. She had known it was over since he told her he was moving to Boston after graduation. Still, she had held on until the end of the school year. *How was I so dumb?*

She realized that all ears were waiting for her reply, so she answered where everyone could hear. "Bradley and I broke up, but truth be known, it had been over for a long time. We both knew it. He was moving to Boston, and I was moving . . ." She hesitated. "I moved home."

They each took turns giving her a long hug before saying goodbye and piling into Kathleen's car. Agnes watched as they blew kisses out the window. Walking back down the dirt lane toward her family's plot number three, she thought about how grateful she was for her friends' love and support.

When she came upon the plot, she was shocked to find the older lady sitting on the tree stump. As Agnes drew near, she could hear the lady talking to the graves. Agnes smiled; she did the same thing when she thought no one else was around. "Good afternoon," Agnes called out as she took the final steps toward her family's plot.

The lady turned slowly, "Hello, Agnes."

"Do I know you?"

"No. But I know you. Your aunt Lottie spoke of you often."

"You knew Lottie?" Agnes asked, thinking she would have known all of Lottie's friends, but then remembered this person was at her funeral. "Of course you did; you are at her funeral."

"Oh yes. We grew up together, but I've lived out of the country for years. I heard of Lottie's passing and was summoned to her funeral."

Agnes nodded, "And you are?"

Gladys locked eyes with Agnes before answering. "My name is Gladys."

Agnes nodded in response before glancing at the tombstone with the same name. *Gladys must have been a popular girl's name at the time*, she thought to herself. "My whole family has been buried here," she told the stranger.

"Oh yes, I knew them all. And I bet I can tell you something you didn't know." Noticing Agnes was intrigued, Gladys continued. "The old family dog is buried right under this old tree stump."

Agnes laughed out loud. "Melvin the Mutt."

Gladys chuckled along with her. "Yes, old Melvin the Mutt. They say he was twenty-five when he finally died."

"I heard thirty," Agnes said, enjoying their banter.

"Maybe you're right. He might have been thirty." Gladys scooted over on the large tree stump and patted beside her. Once Agnes joined her, Gladys offered sympathy for Lottie's death.

Agnes thanked her, then said, "You know, I never realized how much I depended on Lottie. It's strange how all of the stories from our family are gone with her. If a story isn't told, it dies with that person, you know?"

"Yes, I know."

"There are so many things I still need to know."

Gladys thought for a moment. "Maybe I can help you out."

When Agnes opened her mouth to speak, Gladys placed her finger over her lips.

"Maybe I can help you, but not today. I'm tired and need to go rest. Will you come visit me?"

"I'd love that. You said you were from out of town. Will you be staying a while?"

"Yes. I plan to catch up on everything I missed in Savannah, so I rented a place for a few weeks." She scribbled the address on the back of a piece of paper in her purse. "Come one morning after ten." Gladys struggled to get up, but once she did, she stood tall. "Now, don't be out here after dark. The spirits come out."

"That's what Lottie would say."

Gladys tapped Agnes on the end of the nose once more, simply saying, "I know."

8

A CALL HOME

Matthew scanned the faces sitting in the bleachers behind first base. It had been a long three days. Hell, it had been a long three years. After recovering from surgery, he had been persuaded to start running pitching camps for up-and-coming superstars.

He scanned the faces he had gotten to know over the last few days. They were good kids who were all good ball players, but Matthew knew that none of them had what it took.

Over the years, he had only seen a couple of young men who could go the distance. It wasn't for lack of skill. Each one could throw in the upper eighties and low nineties, but it was the lack of spirit. They didn't have the fire in their bellies. Their parents spent a lot of time and money, bought all the right equipment, and they played on all the right travel ball teams. But somewhere between tossing a ball around and competing for a DI scholarship, baseball had become a business instead of a game.

He looked over the players' heads and focused on their parents. Each one anxiously waited to hear that their son was the best. But this time, Matthew would tell them the truth.

"I never remember a time in my life when a baseball wasn't within my reach. I grew up in a neighborhood where there was always someone to throw the ball with. Every day after school, my buddies and I would jump the fence at the nearby field to play ball. Sometimes, we would even play in the lane behind our houses." Matthew paused, letting his memories flood his mind before refocusing. "My mama wanted me to be a priest. She thought if she let me take that scholarship to Notre Dame, I would surely find my calling." He rubbed his hand across his face and mumbled, "Maybe I should have been listening harder."

The man who owned the camp tried to interrupt, but Matthew raised his voice. "You are all wonderful players," he said, looking in the eyes of each of the young men. Then he spoke from his heart. "I want you to take just one thing from this camp. I want you to ask yourself, 'Why do I play baseball?' It's a simple question that gets lost while we are trying to throw the perfect pitch. 'Why do I play baseball?' If your answer is anything other than, 'Because I love the game,' then you need to turn in your glove and leave this game right now."

The parents went crazy, each one yelling in unison to get Matthew's attention. But Matthew ignored them. He turned to the camp owner, whose face was crimson with fury, and said, "I quit!"

On the ride back to his apartment, he thought about everything he needed to do before moving back to Savannah; break the lease to his apartment, turn in his leased car, and turn in his rented furniture. *I have nothing to show for the past three years of my life,* he thought. *I can't keep living with the dream of playing baseball again. I need stability. I need to look to the future. I need Savannah.*

That evening at dinner, he told Camille goodbye. He explained everything to her but added one big thing that was needling in the back of his mind. "My mom's sick, and it seems to be progressing quickly. I think I need to be home."

Camille brought her finger to her lips, deep in thought. Softly, she answered. "I understand you must go, but you will be missed. Greatly. Especially by me." She locked eyes with him as she placed her hand on his knee.

Had he missed the signs? Did she have feelings for him? She had been his physical therapist since he threw out his arm, and they had become friends, but there was no chemistry between them. Besides, she was fifteen years older than him. Surely, she saw that. Still, her next question surprised him.

"What about the wedding?" she asked.

What is she talking about? He searched his mind but came up empty. He sat quietly.

"If you don't want me to come now, I understand," she said. "But I was looking forward to seeing Savannah after you talk about it with such love."

Savannah? Oh, yeah. Jack and Kathleen's wedding. He vaguely remembered their conversation. He had mentioned going home for a wedding, and she had told him she wished she could go to Savannah. He had said, "You're welcome to come with me," but he hadn't thought about it since then. Smiling, he said, "You are welcome to still come."

Her smile grew until she answered, "Okay. I will." For the next hour, they didn't talk about his moving back home. They discussed her flight, Southern weddings, and what she should wear. All guilt of his leaving had been erased.

He asked for the check when he felt the conversation shifting toward his personal life in Savannah. "Okay, then. I have a lot to do before I leave. I guess I'll be seeing you in August." He extended his hand, which she took while pulling herself to stand before him. Staring into his eyes, she whispered, "Goodbye, Matthew," kissing him softly and walking away.

9

THE DANCE

Agnes pulled into the driveway of her Aunt Lottie's house on Isle of Hope. She parked her car on the carport behind the two-bedroom shanty-style house and went through the back door and directly into the kitchen. Breathing in, she thought how much the house still smelled like her Aunt Lottie. Or maybe it was Lottie who had smelled like the house. Would she begin to smell like an old person since she would be living there? And can you actually change the smell of a house? Shaking her head, she knew that wasn't the problem at hand.

Leaving her suitcase in the doorway, she looked around the quaint kitchen. Opening the refrigerator, she expected to find it full of rancid food but only found a few bottles of salad dressing and a jar of strawberry jam. There wasn't a dish in the sink, and the dishwasher had been emptied. Had someone cleaned the house?

Suddenly, the light over the sink flashed on. Agnes looked at the switch in the off position and back up to the light above her.

"Is this how it's gonna be?" Agnes murmured to the quiet house. The house responded by turning the light off.

Leaving the kitchen, she pulled her suitcase out into the hallway. She looked back and forth between bedrooms, trying to decide which one to choose. They were similar in size, but the corner room with two windows won the debate. Tossing her luggage on top of the bed, she made her way onto the large, covered porch that looked over the river. Plopping into a rocker, she closed her eyes and breathed in the smell of the salt marsh.

Can I do this? she wondered. Then, she dug a little deeper into her thoughts. *Do I want to do this? Just because Lottie left me this house and the restaurant doesn't mean I must stay here.* She looked out over the water. It really was a great piece of property. A slow smile moved across her face. *I love Savannah. Why wouldn't I stay here?* She rocked and rocked, remembering her conversations with Lottie on this porch. She had brought many problems to Lottie over the years. But this time, she didn't have Lottie in the chair beside her.

The wind picked up, moving the marsh grass and, in turn, the rocking chair across from her.

"I'm just in the next room," was whispered in her ear, but she wasn't sure if it had been real or imagined. Either way, she decided to enter the conversation.

"The thing is, I didn't have a choice. This was all thrust upon me. I don't mean to be ungrateful, although I now realize I sound that way. But I didn't get to go into the world and choose my future, and now I never will."

An answer popped into her head, the same advice that was given to her one cold night during her freshman year in South Bend when she didn't know if she could stay at Notre Dame.

"Embrace where you are for now. It doesn't mean you'll be there forever. But unless you try what's been laid before you, you'll never know." Picturing Matthew's face made her smile. Although it hadn't ended with Matthew as she had hoped, he had been there for her that night. That moment seemed like forever ago, but it was one of those pivotal moments in her life. A moment when her brain couldn't comprehend the longing in her heart, which was to make her home in South Bend. However, that night lit another longing, too. At the end of their talk, Matthew had pushed a snow-covered piece of hair from her eyes and kissed her softly. The shock of the moment had left an unreadable expression on Matthew's face when he pulled away. She had never experienced anything like it before, and unfortunately, once you experience that feeling, you cannot settle for anything less.

"Embrace where you are for now." She nodded, acknowledging her decision. "It's time to make this place my home," she said into the breeze. "And this time, by choice."

She suddenly realized darkness had set in. It happened so quickly with her eyes focused on the horizon. She remembered the small lamp on the table beside her, so she flipped it on. Then she noticed the old boombox sitting beside the lamp. "Let's see what you were listening to," she whispered and pressed PLAY. Immediately, the beginning melody from the song "At Last" by Etta James began to fill her surroundings.

Memories of dancing with Lottie around the porch encircled her. She had always been more introverted than others. Playing basketball had kept her in shape, but it also made her more muscular than her friends, which made her feel less feminine. However, Lottie could always get her up and dancing. She smiled, remembering Lottie's phrase, "Dance like no one is watching," and she did just that.

She moved and spun as the song progressed, with not one worry in her mind. When the last stanza of the song began, she sang along.

You smiled, you smiled
Oh, and then the spell was cast

And here we are in Heaven
For you are mine at last

She swayed to the end of the melody, picturing Lottie and Benjamin dancing to the song. Nodding to the image of them enjoying it together once again, she turned off the light and stood motionless, looking out over the marsh.

The rustling sound of the breeze chasing the marsh grass got her attention, and somewhere further inland, she heard the trotting of a horse. "Strange," she whispered. She had never seen horses on Isle of Hope, but somehow the mingling of the sounds soothed her. She took in the smells and sounds around her one last time, then went inside to unpack her clothes and settle into her new life.

The sound of carbonation escaping his ice-cold PBR was like music to his ears. Matthew smiled, eagerly anticipating his first sip. It had been a long day packing shrimp and icing down seafood. He was grateful to finally be back on the sailboat to relax.

He scanned the Isle of Hope bluff slowly, beginning at the marina and then studying each house along the bank until he ended at his favorite, the small cottage at the point. He had grown up running the streets on the island; his grandparents owned one of the center houses sitting on the bluff. He came from "old money," but over time, he realized that statement meant that the old generation had the money. Thankfully, the house was what remained of the fortune his great-grandfather made with the railroad. His parents now lived there. He focused on their home, searching for movement, but his eyes moved on when he didn't see any.

He knew most of the houses along the bluff. His grandfather loved walking with him and pointing out the various houses. Each had a unique story about who once lived inside and their success or demise.

Matthew's gaze was fixed on the little cottage at the tip. He wondered, not for the first time, what happened to the nice lady who once lived there. His eyes were focused on the cottage when, surprisingly, a light popped on, casting a spider-like outline of the oaks along the bluff. It was strange that he hadn't noticed any lights in the cottage since moving onto the sailboat.

The sound of music reached his ears. He could barely make out the song but recognized Etta James belting out, "At Last." Turning his head, he strained to listen to the music and was thankful that the sound carried so easily across the open marsh. He closed his eyes and pictured a ninety-year-old lady sitting on the porch, bobbing her rocking chair while reminiscing with a song that once meant a lot to her and someone special. When the song ended, he looked back to the house and noticed movement on the porch. The picture of the elderly lady was instantly replaced by a young woman spinning to the music.

"I should look away," he said to himself, but he was mesmerized by her gentle sway. He hadn't realized he had been holding his breath until he exhaled. He searched the porch for her dance partner. "Please don't let a mister be sitting on that porch with her," he mumbled as the song ended. Shamefully, he continued to stare until her dancing came to an end. Once she stopped, she stood in place for the longest time, peering over the marsh. *Does she see me?* He wondered selfishly but knew no lights were burning on his sailboat.

Everything went dark when she turned off the light that had been coming from a small lamp on the porch, but somehow, he could still feel her presence. Or maybe he was hoping she was still there. Seconds passed, then minutes, while he stared at the spot that last held movement. The sound of a screen door banging shut put an end to his trance as the moment passed from the present to a memory.

"You sure wouldn't see something like that in Chicago," he thought as a slow smile crossed his face. He stretched back against the boat cushions and stared into a night full of stars. For the first time since he had been home, he looked forward to finding out what Savannah had in store for him.

10

THE CRYSTAL

Agnes merged into the flow of traffic circling around Pulaski Square. Scanning the road ahead like an eagle searching for its next meal, she smiled when she noticed a couple climbing into their car across the park. Stepping on the gas, she maneuvered quickly toward the spot, only to get stuck behind a minivan. "Go, Go, Go," she uttered impatiently while slowly closing the distance to the coveted space. As she drove around the last corner, the van pulled head-first into the spot, leaving its tail hanging in the road. "Rookie," she said under her breath while she patiently watched the gentleman switch from drive to reverse several times before he finally parked the car.

Agnes passed by slowly, trying to catch a glimpse of its driver, and was rewarded when both he and his passenger waved as she passed.

Agnes continued to drive toward the Crystal Beer Parlor and luckily found a spot right out front on Jefferson. She smiled as she approached the building's angled entrance.

Several of the historic Savannah buildings constructed on intersections had corner doors. Like this one, most had been built to be a grocery store. But what was once a store in the early 1900s metamorphosized into a beautiful restaurant in the 1930s known as The Crystal, Savannah's oldest restaurant? However, her friends knew it as the home of Savannah's best burger.

Since the tribe was finally back together again, they decided to start meeting every Wednesday at 11:30 for lunch. Each lady took turns choosing the restaurant, making it a competition to see who had chosen the best. Today, Jan's choice was the Crystal Beer Parlor.

She found her friends sitting in a large booth beside the bar, perusing the menu with cocktails in hand. They all looked up at the same time with welcoming smiles. She paused, thinking how nice it was to be loved unconditionally by five amazing women like her friends.

"We took the liberty of ordering you a drink," Jan announced.

"Perfect," Agnes responded, noticing the copper mug holding a Moscow Mule. "I know it's not even twelve, but I could use a drink."

All eyes were on Agnes, so she held her drink in the air, "Cheers!"

The table responded with "Cheers!" and each took a sip.

"I never really understood 'Cheers.' Do you take a sip afterward to respond, or can you just hold up your glass?" Stephanie asked.

They each looked around the table, waiting for someone to answer. Eventually, all eyes settled on Kathleen.

"Okay, I'm going out on a limb here, but you're raising your glass as a toast, and a toast is followed by a sip. When my dad made a toast at home, he would hold up his glass, make a statement, and then say, 'Sláinte.' We would reply with 'Sláinte,' and then everyone would sip their beverage to honor the toast. So yes, let's end it with a sip."

And just like that, the matter was settled. And just like always, Kathleen was the one to settle it. They were having a happy conversation when the waitress came to the table. "You are a lively bunch this morning," she said, checking her watch to verify the time. After taking their order, she brought two baskets of cornbread, saying, "I sure wish my friends would get together like this."

They smiled at one another, soaking in the compliment, then began going around the table, catching up.

Latrice explained, "It's been so hard settling back into Savannah after living abroad for so many years. I'm really trying to regain my footing." She paused briefly, then asked Agnes, "How are you adjusting to being home?"

Agnes thought before answering. When she spoke, her voice cracked. "I love being back in Savannah, but..." She let the but hang in the air while she tried to put her thoughts into words. "You all knew my Aunt Lottie." They all nodded their heads. "And you all knew she was...well, let's just say she was eccentric."

Stephanie interjected, "If eccentric means psychic, yes, she was." Everyone nodded in agreement.

Kathleen reached out and placed her hand on Agnes. "Your Aunt had special gifts and used them well."

"Yes, she did. But I still don't understand why she left me all she did. I have a restaurant sitting vacant, just waiting for me to decide how to proceed. And I'm living in a house that I know Lottie still wanders around in."

"Why do you think that?" Stephanie asked.

"Well, I only moved in on Monday, but lights come on and off, cabinets and doors sometimes open and close, and I found a box on my kitchen table this morning—just out of the blue."

Maggie spoke up. "Was it there when you moved in?"

"No. Well, I don't think so."

"Damn," Latrice blurted out.

"The thing is, I'm in control of my own destiny. Not Lottie or anyone else." Everyone nodded with encouragement. "I moved home and inherited Lottie's estate. I don't mean to sound ungrateful, but this was not what I planned for my future. I could sell everything and just walk away. But if I choose to stay in Savannah, I'll reopen the restaurant. It intrigues me. I've been doing some research and figuring out a business plan. She has the main oyster stew business that basically runs itself, and I think I could do well opening for breakfast and coffee. What are your thoughts?"

Everyone chimed in with approval. So, Agnes agreed. "All right then, I choose Aggie's."

"Aggie's? Where is that?" Jan asked.

Agnes smiled, "It's my new restaurant. And guess what, next week is my turn to choose what restaurant we eat in, and I choose mine. I'll see you at 11:30 for a late brunch. Come hungry."

For the first time since she moved back to Savannah, she had a plan and was excited about the future.

11

GLADYS

Agnes walked sleepily onto the porch with her first cup of coffee. The smell of her dark roast mingling with the salty marsh made her sigh with delight. She couldn't think of a better way to spend her first full morning in her new house.

She sat on the old metal glider that had been in the same spot for thirty years and focused on a new sailboat moored in the creek. *When did you get here? I didn't see you there when I went to bed.* She thought, then watched it intently. She had always envied people who could sail. The last time she was on a sailboat was in tenth grade when a guy she had a crush on asked her to ride with him to bring his boss' boat into dry dock in Thunderbolt. Her friend had figured the tides incorrectly, and the tall mast of the boat got stuck while trying to pass under the Islands Expressway Bridge. The fast-moving tide carried the boat forward as the mast slowly broke in half, leaving lines and sails flying everywhere. When they finally made it to the dock, her young friend had been so shaken up that he ran to the nearest phone and called his mom, leaving her alone on the boat. She had walked around the marina and had recognized a couple in a sailboat who were friends with her mom. She paused for a minute, pondering that moment. That couple had been Matthew's parents. They had been on their sailboat. The one that had a long green stripe down its side.

Her eyes flew open and focused on the sailboat in the channel, noticing its long green stripe.

"Well, I'll be damned. What are the odds of that?" she said aloud. "I wonder why they are mooring their sailboat in Isle of Hope?" She watched quietly for another moment as the sun made its way into the sky, wondering what it might feel like to wake up on a boat. Her stomach lurched in response. She was cursed with terrible motion sickness and never wanted to find out the answer to that question, but the pain in her stomach was followed by a silence-breaking growl.

The smell of cinnamon floated through the bright blue screen door. Although it was warped from the salt water, it still let fresh air in the house without the many bugs who chose to live in Savannah. But this morning, the screen door was letting out the evidence of her early morning baking.

She had woken up early to the sound of horses and couldn't go back to sleep. So, she had done the one thing that always seemed to ease her mind: bake. The cinnamon buns had become something that was easy to bake, and everybody seemed to enjoy them. She made a batch to walk over to Gladys a bit later. Now that her stomach was talking to her, she decided to have one with her coffee.

The screen door screeched behind her when she entered the house. That had become the case for most things in her new home. Each one showed its age. They were still usable—in fact, they were sturdier than most things today. But, just like an old man trying to tie his shoes, the tired house would moan under strain.

"Thank you, old girl," Agnes replied to the creaks and

cracks. They made the house almost feel alive and always warmed her heart.

Walking into the kitchen, she first noticed the box with her name still sitting on the table. She had walked by the box several times that week, but this time, the box seemed to be sitting on the table's edge. How could that be? It couldn't, of course. She waved it off and walked toward the sticky buns, but once she placed one on her plate, her eyes drifted back to the box.

"Maybe it's time," Agnes said to the box. She grabbed her plate and settled into the kitchen chair. Slowly tracing the cursive lines of each letter of her name on the top of the box seemed to give her ownership of its contents, so she opened the lid without any reservations. The packing of the box had been well thought out and stacked according to size. Things that were meant to be together were tied with pale blue grosgrain ribbon, and loose papers had been clipped together.

She quickly viewed the deed to the house, the title of the car, the business plan for the restaurant, and general directions on how to run the house. The next thing she pulled from a padded white envelope was a key ring that read "Shed" and had many keys hanging from it. The envelope on the very bottom had a handwritten note scribbled on the outside with the statement Lottie had told her in the cemetery just months before. "You will learn many things over the next year." Inside the envelope was a simple address and many black and white photos. Agnes flipped through them all. She could make out Lottie and her grandmother, Elizabeth, but all the other faces and locations were a mystery. She pulled the piece of paper out of the stack of pictures and read the address to the end. Puzzled, she whispered, "I wonder what's on Prince Edward Island?" Then added, "I wonder where Prince Edward Island is?"

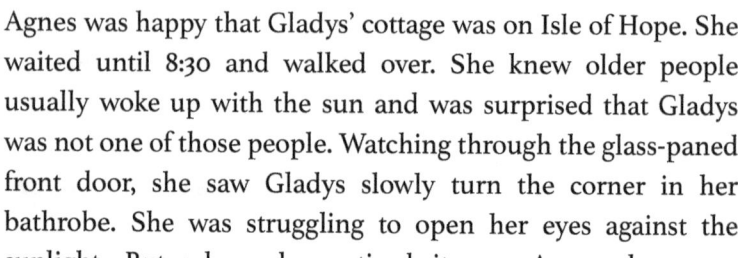

Agnes was happy that Gladys' cottage was on Isle of Hope. She waited until 8:30 and walked over. She knew older people usually woke up with the sun and was surprised that Gladys was not one of those people. Watching through the glass-paned front door, she saw Gladys slowly turn the corner in her bathrobe. She was struggling to open her eyes against the sunlight. But when she noticed it was Agnes, her pace quickened.

As she opened the door, Agnes announced, "I brought you something."

Gladys sniffed the air. "I smell something yummy. What do you have there?"

"I couldn't sleep, so I started baking early this morning," she said, not mentioning the sound of horses that had startled her out of her sleep.

Gladys led her to the kitchen, and they sat at a small wooden table. When Agnes opened the container lid to show off her sticky buns, Gladys let out a long whistle. "I'm going to need a cup of coffee with those beauties."

Agnes watched her as she moved toward the coffee pot. Gladys reminded her so much of Lottie, but Agnes wasn't sure why. They didn't look alike at all, but something was the same. Agnes smiled at the two curls around her face that were still pinned down from the night before. Lottie did the same thing. She wondered if older people just had certain habits that were all the same, but then Gladys said her name.

"Agnes, how do you take your coffee?"

It was as if Lottie had said her name aloud. Their voices were the same. She had to hear it again, so she asked, "What?" and then closed her eyes.

"How do you take your coffee?"

This time, there was no trace of Lottie. "Cream and sugar, please," Agnes answered.

They sat and chit-chatted about nothing special, just enjoying each other's company. When Agnes finally stood to pour herself another cup of coffee, she brought Gladys' cup with her to refill. "Now it's my turn. How do you take your coffee?" she asked.

"I take mine with just a teaspoon of vanilla extract."

Agnes paused. *Just like Lottie took hers*, she thought and immediately heard Lottie say, "There's no such thing as coincidences."

As their time together came to an end, Gladys asked, "I was wondering if you would be able to help me with something. I wanted to go to Tybee, but I thought it might be too far for me to drive. Could you take me there?"

Agnes agreed. "Sure. I have some things to do in the morning at work, but why don't you meet me around lunch, and we can go from there."

12

TURNER CREEK

Agnes was busy unpacking boxes at the restaurant when she heard a knock on the back door but was happy when she opened it to Gladys.

"I brought you a little present," Gladys announced, passing her a perfectly wrapped box.

"Come on in," Agnes said, holding the door open for Gladys. "It's chilly today."

Gladys nodded and walked further into the kitchen. Pointing to a small table covered with papers and bills, she asked, "May I sit?"

"Of course," Agnes answered, quickly gathering the scattered papers. Once she sat down, she opened the present and held up the stark white apron with "Agnes" monogrammed across the front. "I love it. Thank you so much."

Gladys sat up proudly. "Every great chef needs a great apron."

"Well, I don't know about being great, but I sure am looking forward to trying," Agnes answered. She watched as Gladys surveyed the kitchen, taking in every inch of it. She never took off her jacket and sat with her purse in her lap. *I can read the signs*, Agnes thought. "Are you ready for our adventure?" she asked, then laughed when Gladys was up and at the door almost before Agnes finished her sentence.

On the drive to Tybee, Gladys pointed out how things once looked. She told Agnes about the great Savannah car race that ran down Victory Drive and through Isle of Hope. She explained where restaurants and banks once were and asked Agnes about the establishments that had replaced them. She had a story about everything. They traveled over the Thunderbolt Bridge toward Tybee, but when the road split at Johnny Mercer Boulevard, Gladys yelled out, "Turn." So, Agnes turned.

"Why do you want to drive down Johnny Mercer?" Agnes asked.

"Is there another way to go?" Gladys asked.

"Yes. But we can still go this way. And it's much prettier."

"This way was the only way to Tybee for as long as I knew," Gladys remarked, letting her eyes explore everything on the way. "It's now called Johnny Mercer, you say? I met him once on one of his visits home; he was a hoot. And look at this road now. It only had two small lanes when I lived here. Oh, and the oaks filled in nicely. Their overhang makes me feel like I'm in a tunnel."

Gladys continued a rolling commentary until the car approached the Turner Creek Bridge. She suddenly stopped talking. The quiet got Agnes' attention, and when she glanced at Gladys, she noticed her hands shaking. "What's wrong?" she asked.

"Can you pull over?"

"Absolutely, just let me get over Turner Creek," Agnes answered. She changed lanes and pulled off the road into the pharmacy's parking lot, which was backed up to the marsh.

Gladys opened her door. Leaving it hanging open, she began to walk towards the marsh line. Agnes jumped out and followed closely behind. Gladys pushed through the pharmacy's landscaped bushes, then over bramble, right to the marsh's edge. She walked until her shoes began to sink into the mud. Her thoughts raced back to the most terrifying time of her life, back to the night that she died.

She was startled when Agnes touched her hand, and then she gripped it for dear life.

"I struggled to carry the three bottles down the dock. I was relieved when I stepped across the gangway and onto the vessel. It was a beauty, with scrubbed white decks and glassy, stained wood trim. I wondered who was lucky enough to be on board, and I searched for someone to leave the champagne with, but no one was in sight. I heard voices toward the back of the yacht and happily ducked through the open doorway to follow them back. But when I got closer, I saw three men kneeling near the back rail. They were gagged and bound. Their faces were bloodied and bruised as their attacker went from one to the other, just pounding them."

Gladys took a deep breath but was still in the moment, retelling something she had witnessed a lifetime ago. She continued, "I had to get out of there, but I couldn't take my eyes off the three men. I slowly began to back away as the gun exploded, and the first man collapsed onto the floor. I told myself to run, but my whole body was shaking too hard. I forced myself to tip-toe backward. Then the second gunshot pierced the air." Gladys began to sob.

"Let's go back to the car, Gladys," Agnes suggested, but Gladys didn't hear one word Agnes said; she was lost in another time.

"I knew people would hear the gunshots and come rescue me, but at that moment, I heard the fireworks exploding overhead. The captors had planned it perfectly. When I turned to run, my movement caught the eye of that last man. He looked at me, pleading, when the gun exploded in his face. But his eyes had given me away. I watched as that same gun spun in my direction, but thankfully, my feet began to move.

"They screamed to each other to kill me. I still remember their voices. They were scared. I had seen too much. So, when I reached the open deck of the yacht, I dove into the Wilmington River. I held my breath as long as I could, swimming with all my might to escape. When I came up, I didn't know where I was until the light from a firework exploded overhead. It helped me focus on the marsh line. I could hear the men yelling to each other from the dock, but the swift incoming tide pulled me away."

Gladys' voice trailed off until she stood motionless, looking out towards the river. The cold water seeping into her shoes snapped Gladys back to reality, and she took a shaky breath. She glanced down at her hand holding Agnes' and then looked into Agnes' face, expelling a deep sigh. "I haven't been back to Wilmington Island since that night."

Agnes squeezed her hand but noticed Gladys was shivering. The water from the marsh had soaked the bottom of her pants, and her lips were turning blue. "Let's go back to the car, okay?"

Gladys nodded and let Agnes lead her. When she was settled back in her seat, Agnes started the car and turned on the heat.

"I think I need to get you home, Gladys," Agnes reasoned and began driving off Wilmington Island, backtracking the way they came.

They drove without saying a word, but as they approached Thunderbolt, Gladys began talking again. She picked up right where she had left off. "I'm thankful I was a strong swimmer, so I swam with the current coming into Turner's Creek. The river runs quickly, so eventually, all I had to do was float. I decided to get out at the bridge. Right where we were just standing. My uncle Carl was the Bridge Attendant, so I knew I'd be safe if I could get to him. I didn't think about crossing the marsh. When

I tried to pull up to stand, the mud sucked my feet right down to my knees. I struggled slowly towards the bank, only yelling out once when my heel got sliced on an oyster bar. When I finally made it to the road, I waited. The bridge attendant's office sat in the middle of the bridge, and it was at least a fifty-yard stretch of open space to get to the top. I didn't know how bad my foot was cut until I began to run. Oh, the pain it sent. The cut was so deep my heel flapped. But I knew how far I'd come to get away from those killers, and I knew they'd be looking for me. I couldn't give up."

"I heard the car before I saw its lights and tried as hard as I could to run faster. I watched the climb of the headlights rising along the bridge, and they were almost upon me. I looked ahead at the office and noticed the door was wide open, probably trying to get cool air on the hot July night. As the light from the car was inches from my heels, I dove into the room. The car continued over the bridge, but I damn near gave my uncle a heart attack. Terror hit his face when he saw my bloodied, muddy self, but he stayed calm. I was able to tell him men were trying to kill me for something I saw, before I passed out. The next thing I remember is riding in the car with him toward Boston and him telling me I was safe. That's the night that Gladys Hughes died."

They didn't say a word the rest of the way; they just held hands. When they pulled into the restaurant parking lot, Agnes turned the engine off and spun towards Gladys. "You're Lottie's sister?" she asked. Gladys nodded but continued to stare ahead blankly. Agnes added, "I'm so sorry, Aunt Gladys. You lost so much."

Gladys turned and wrapped her arms around Agnes. *She has no idea how much I lost*, Gladys thought. Still, this was not the time to explain. She knew she must speak to Agnes' mother first, but right now, in her mind, she was still floating down Turner Creek, struggling for her life.

13

WEDDING BELLS

Agnes walked through the large mahogany doors of the Cathedral of Saint John the Baptist. She scanned the crowd, looking for the tribe, but instead made eye contact with Matthew. How could she have forgotten that he and Jack were good friends? She felt the immediate blush in her cheeks as a slow smile spread across his face. She began to walk towards him when the moment was quickly interrupted by a tug on his jacket.

Agnes' gaze shifted to the tall blonde at his side while the Amazonian beauty sized her up. Agnes stopped dead in her tracks as she watched Matthew's escort whisper into his ear. *Like I care that Matthew is partial to blondes with tanned legs up to their ears*, she thought to herself. So, she changed directions and went in search of the tribe.

Kathleen was talking with her mother in the back of the church. She waved Agnes over and pointed to the other four bridesmaids gathered around the baptismal Font. The six of them had been friends since their first day in high school when they found themselves sitting at the same table in the St. Vincent's Academy lunchroom. They had stayed close, even though they had each gone their separate ways after graduation. Thankfully, each one of them was home for the summer.

Kathleen was the mom of the group, so it was no surprise she would be the first to marry. Although she had just returned from a graduation trip to Ireland, she had been completely organized and had left each of them a list to be done for the wedding.

"Did you finally get in touch with Brother Thackery about the special arrangement of flowers to be left at Our Lady's altar?" Jan asked Agnes as she approached.

"Yes, he said he would leave a vase to set them in," Agnes answered. Jan was an artist, so it was no surprise that she was worried about flowers. Agnes motioned toward Jack and his friends. "So, who are our groomsmen?"

Latrice piped in, "One is your brother, Chris. He sure has filled in nicely over the past four years, if you know what I mean."

"Oh my gosh!" Agnes nudged her with her elbow. "You're talking about my brother." They all laughed, so she got up the courage to ask, "Who is that with Matthew?"

"He brought her home with him from Chicago," Maggie answered.

"Girlfriend?" Agnes asked further.

"Don't know. I thought you weren't interested in Matthew anymore."

"I'm not interested, just curious," Agnes answered.

"Yeah, right. We've seen that 'curious' look before, like when you were 'curious' about Eddie Fox and asked him to the Ring Dance," Stephanie said while trying to tighten a loose finial on the handrail.

"Good Ole Eddie. He taught me all his really cool dance moves that night," Agnes answered as she began to do the wave with her hands. They all started the wave along with her as Kathleen approached.

"Why are we dancing like Eddie?" Kathleen asked Agnes, making the group laugh.

"I was simply asking about Matthew. I should have known better," Agnes answered.

"Ah, Matthew. The one of Jack's groomsmen who traveled the furthest to get here. Matthew came in for the week to be at the wedding and to visit his family. His mom was just diagnosed with a degenerative muscle disease and really wants him to move back to Savannah."

"And his arm candy?" Stephanie asked.

"He said she's just a friend who wanted to see Savannah, but she seems to think otherwise. Guys are so clueless."

All six of them stared at the couple while discussing his relationship status. Matthew's "friend" turned towards them, smiled, and slid her hand into the crook of Matthew's jacket.

"Snap!" Latrice said while snapping her fingers in unison. "We just got caught."

"Yes, we did, and we know better. You always turn your back to the people you're talking about," Maggie explained.

"Or you don't talk about people at all," Kathleen chided.

They were interrupted when Father Sullivan called the group together. He welcomed them to the rehearsal and lined everyone up to practice the procession. He had the bridesmaids and groomsmen all line up according to their height and then process one by one. After everyone was at the altar, they practiced each part of the Mass, such as when to sit and stand. Then, the bridesmaids processed out on the arm of their coordinating groomsmen. Agnes groaned when she realized she was with Matthew.

He offered his elbow to help her down the stairs of the altar, and she ran her hand inside. Walking down the aisle, he began, "So, I hear you had to move home."

Somehow, his statement angered her. "Had to" implied that she had no choice, which made her mad. "I sure did," she answered, then angrily added, "And I hear you won't move home." Why she said it, she had no idea. It was hateful and gossip.

He stopped, which stopped the whole procession. "Where did you hear that from?"

She looked back to the altar, where Father Sullivan motioned for them to keep moving. "I think we need to move along," she said as she tugged his elbow, but Matthew stood in place, waiting for an answer.

"Answer me. Who told you that?" he asked again.

"It's just the word on the street," she whispered.

"And when did you start believing the word on the street?" he asked accusingly.

Agnes tugged one last time on his elbow, but he pulled away. She shook her head and continued walking toward the back of the church without her escort.

Father Sullivan was the last person to process out. He gathered the group and addressed them, "Let's run through that one more time." Pointing to Agnes, he continued, "This time without interruption."

They began going through the rehearsal again. This time, as they processed out, arm in arm, Matthew and Agnes didn't utter a word to one another. When they cleared the massive mahogany doors in the rear, Agnes quickly removed her hand from Matthew's arm. She was surprised when he grabbed it. When she turned to him to protest, he squared her gaze and said, "Not that it's any of your business, but I moved home last month to be with my family. You can share that with all your little gossiping friends."

She watched him walk away, ashamed of herself for repeating gossip and also for judging him.

As Jan's escort dropped her at the back of the line, she turned to Agnes and asked, "What just happened?"

"I just got told. That's what happened. And I deserved it."

14

THE CHAPEL

Agnes laced up her shoes and threw on a ball cap. She had only been home for a few months but noticed her clothes hugging her a little tighter than before. At first, she blamed it on her activity level. She had been very active at school on the basketball team. But the truth of the matter was that food was better in the South. They put more emphasis on their seasonings and presentation.

When she was in Indiana, she missed her mom's cooking. But really, she missed the southern flavors. People teased that she liked everything fried, but more than that, she craved the seasonings. She had grown up in her mom's kitchen and Lottie's restaurant. She had a flare for Southern cuisine and loved seafood. That's what she had missed the most. Shrimp, scallops, and oysters were hard to find in her college town. But now that she was home, she would keep them close at hand.

She played around with various recipes at the restaurant, still trying to perfect the menu. Every time she made a change, she would call her friends to come try the new dish. But the one thing she didn't touch was Lottie's oyster stew recipe. Lottie made different versions of it, but the original version was the best seller. The stew was added to the menu every September and remained there until April. Lottie had even added extra refrigerators to store the mussels.

Agnes never knew the oysters could remain alive in cold storage for weeks if kept damp. For some reason, she thought that they had to be eaten or cooked immediately after they were plucked from the salt water. It wasn't until that past summer that Lottie had given Agnes a lesson on oysters.

Holding the oyster still in its shell, she reviewed what Agnes knew about shucking. Once the oyster was open, she sucked it down raw.

"Don't you add anything like lemon or cocktail sauce?" Agnes had asked.

"No, sir-re-bob. That only covers up the natural flavors. You know, you can taste the difference between a Savannah oyster and oysters in other parts of the world. Savannah oysters are known to have a saltier lemongrass flavor. That's why they are so good in my stew. Always remember that."

Agnes smiled at the memory of them eating oysters in the kitchen that day. It had been one of those days when you were supposed to be doing something important but spent the day doing something altogether different, like when you were preparing for an important project and instead cleaned the grout on your bathroom floor that had been dirty for three years. That was one of those days, and it was spent with Lottie schooling Agnes about the importance of oysters in Savannah. But more so than that, it had been the passing on of good Southern food from one generation to the next. But right now, that next generation couldn't button her jeans.

She knew the route she would take because she wanted to see what was on the other side of her property. She began walking the streets that ran along the marsh, winding then turning around when she hit dead-end roads. She had known the stories of the land being settled by General Oglethorpe's surveyor, by the name of Noble Jones, in the early 1700s. Lottie had a coffee-table book with the island's history. The French originally found the island and named it L'Isle Desperance. Roughly translated, it meant Isle of Hope. Over time, it had become just that. Savannah families would move out of the city to escape the summer's heat. Later, they would retreat from the city, running from malaria outbreaks. She had read all about the famous Bluff Drive and even old Camp Villa Marie, but Isle of Hope was a much larger island than what she expected.

She jogged slowly around the island, then circled back towards the marina. Cutting over on a crush-and-run lane, she saw the Catholic chapel. She remembered walking over with Lottie for Masses and wanted to sneak a peek. Looking down at her running clothes, she began to question her appearance. But no cars were parked in the small lot, so she proceeded.

Opening the chapel doors, she was met by the sound of the recitation of the Rosary. All heads turned to look at her while they continued saying a Hail Mary. Agnes began to slowly back out, but several of the ladies waved her inside, so she proceeded through the door and slid into the back pew. The group was reciting the fifth mystery, so she jumped in. When they made the final Sign of the Cross, Agnes rose and walked toward the door.

She felt a hand on her shoulder, followed by a small voice. "Agnes? Is that you?"

Turning, she was met by the gentle eyes of Matthew's mother. Although Agnes had heard she had been sick, Mrs. Monroe looked young and spry. "Hello, Mrs. Monroe. How are you?"

"I'm just fine, dear. Matthew told me you were back in town. I'm happy that you popped into our rosary group this morning."

"I'm sorry I interrupted. I was walking by and wanted to

come inside. I came to the chapel with my Aunt Lottie a few times and I wanted to peek inside."

"Please don't rush off. Come and meet the group," she said while pulling Agnes' hand towards the front of the chapel where the ladies had accumulated after the Rosary. "Everybody, this is Agnes, Lottie's niece." That statement got their full attention, and everybody turned to welcome her to the group. They began pelting her with questions.

"Are you back in Savannah to stay?"

"How is the restaurant coming?

And then the one question that stopped her in her tracks: "Do you share the same gifts as your Aunt Lottie?"

Agnes searched the group for the owner of the quiet voice who had just asked the question and found a petite lady sitting near the back. They locked eyes, and Agnes nodded at her. She answered the other questions and then told the group she was happy to meet them before making her way to the lady in the back. People said their goodbyes on their way out, until finally, it was just Agnes and the small lady.

Agnes introduced herself, and they shook hands. "Unfortunately, I do not share the same gifts as my aunt. There was no one like Lottie. I'm happy you knew her so well."

The petite woman wiped a tear back from her face. "Me, too," she replied.

Agnes patted the woman's hand, then stood to leave, but the woman pulled her back down.

"Lottie helped me talk to my husband. He's been gone for two years and three months, and he left me with so many questions."

"I'm very sorry for your loss," Agnes replied.

"Lottie said he was only in the next room. But I must admit, I don't really understand that analogy."

Agnes leaned in and whispered in her ear. "Lottie would tell me that same line, 'He's only in the next room.' It's very confusing to us normal people."

The lady held her rosary beads up for Agnes to view. "Lottie always wanted to hold something of mine, something that had been blessed and was special to me. When she held these, she would answer the question swirling in my mind. It was spectacular."

She placed the rosary beads into Agnes' hand. They were warm. No, they were hot. Agnes wondered how they held the heat from the lady's hands. Turning to the lady, Agnes whispered, "Small red box in the drawer under the stove." She wasn't sure why she blurted that out or what it even meant, but the lady understood it all too well.

"Oh my," was all that the widow said.

Agnes sat wide-eyed, looking into the distance, repeating the woman's sentiment. "Yes, oh my!"

15

SAVANNAH ARCHIVES

Gladys had been disoriented her first few days back in Savannah, grieving the city she had lost. Everything in Savannah had changed, so much so that she barely recognized it at all. It didn't help that nearly all the people she had once known were gone, too. *They all died thinking I was dead. How crazy is that?*

She had never asked Lottie about what had happened the days, weeks, and months after she went missing. A part of her didn't even want to know. She couldn't bear to hear how her parents had suffered. She had now lost a child, too. *Your heart never heals from that loss, and I caused that for my parents.* She wondered, not for the first time, if she had made the right choice in fleeing, but once again pictured the three men being shot in the head, one by one. Either way, she would have been dead, and most likely, her family, too.

In her second week back in Savannah, Gladys got up the nerve to discover what happened after her disappearance. She made an appointment with the Savannah archivist, who asked for her specific needs. "I'd like to look through newspaper articles beginning in July 1938."

The nice lady didn't seem to be curious at all. She probably got random requests every day. She simply stated, "Follow me," and led Gladys to a small room with a microfilm machine. The archivist began to search while explaining to Gladys how to retrieve the newspaper from each day and how to print things she found.

"Printing is five cents a copy, and I will be counting how many copies you make," the lady snipped. Gladys nodded quickly, like a schoolgirl in trouble, which made the lady smile in response. As she left, she pulled the door shut behind her.

It didn't take long for Gladys to find what she was looking for. In the July 3rd edition of *The Savannah Evening Press*, there was a long article titled "Robbery at Sea."

On July 2nd, the yacht of one of New England's wealthiest families, William Sandry, was robbed. The yacht, Sandry Sun, was traveling to Miami when it was overtaken by three masked thieves at gunpoint just off the coast of Tybee Island, Georgia. The family and crew were unharmed, but the thieves made off with diamonds, registered jewels, and family heirlooms.

Gladys printed the article. She had always wondered about the jewels, and now she knew who they belonged to. As she returned to scanning, she stopped briefly to read the following article.

Man arrested in Laurel Grove Cemetery.

Treasure hunter Ian Whiting was arrested yesterday after being discovered digging around the graves of Confederate colonels. "The treasure is there, I know it," he told a Savannah News reporter.

Gladys rolled her eyes and muttered, "No, it's not, Ian. It doesn't exist. It never did." Shaking her head, she moved to articles from the following day. The headline from July 5 made her breath catch.

Local girl missing from the annual General Oglethorpe Hotel's July 4th party

Gladys Hughes went missing on July 4th from the General Oglethorpe Hotel, where she worked for the summer. Witnesses placed her on the dock and have begun to question whether she possibly fell and hit her head. A search crew is still looking for her. Any information will be appreciated. Pictured below are her father, the hotel's operating manager, and her two sisters, who were working the same shift.

Gladys struggled to swallow. The tormented look on their faces broke her heart. She zoomed in on her father. Strange that he looked so young. She had never watched him age. In her mind, he was forever forty-five. The cry in her throat broke through to whimpering tears. She quickly wiped her eyes to clear her vision so she could see the "Print" button, then moved to the following day's newspaper. Day after day, the search crew scanned the creeks and marshes, interviewing boaters who had been at the festivities and guests who had been at the hotel.

The only guest interview that had been printed was from a man whose face she remembered. But now she had a name to put with it. Ron Graci. That face. She would never forget that face. It was the face of the man who had been sent to silence her. She had seen too much. "Get her, Ronny. Don't let her get away," Ron's boss had cried out. She could still hear his voice in her mind. Her trembling hands wouldn't allow her to hit "Print" this time. Rubbing them round and round slowly made them steady once again, allowing her to read the entire article.

"This story is coming to you from the General Oglethorpe Hotel where we were able to interview guest, Ron Graci. He gave us a new approach to Gladys Hughes' disappearance.

"We ordered champagne to drink while enjoying the fireworks, but it never showed. We never saw the girl."

She continued to scan the papers until she stopped suddenly. The hair on her arms stood at attention when she read the headline for July 25th. "Savannah mourns the death of Gladys Hughes." This time, the waterworks flowed non-stop with pictures and sentiments of so many people. She slowly reviewed each photo, printing the ones she wanted to keep. The picture of poor Uncle Carl gripped her heart. She made a mental note to search for his obituary so she could visit his grave.

She continued looking at the pictures, stopping on one with her old St. Vincent's high school friends. She zoomed in and leaned closer to the computer. Over one of the young lady's head was none other than Ron Graci, standing in the back beside a tree. He had been searching for her for years. It must have thrilled him when he finally found her.

She searched for another roll of microfilm and put it in the machine. It didn't take much time to find yet another headline.

Local Man Shoots Intruder.

The Savannah Police Department was called by several Isle of Hope residents to investigate the sound of gunshots being fired from Mystic Lane. Police found local Benjamin Foster with his hysterical wife, Lottie. They reported that their Isle of Hope house had been broken into while they slept, and her husband, Benjamin Foster, had shot and killed a known felon, Mr. Ron Graci.

Gladys replayed the night in her mind. Wasn't it ironic that Ron Graci died the same way he had killed those poor three boaters; a bullet to the head. She knew this because she was there and saw the whole thing.

16

OYSTERING

Matthew watched for the dancing lady almost every night. For whatever reason, she eased his pain of coming home from work tired and hot. His daily aggravation changed to the anticipation of seeing her once again. But over the course of the week, the porch remained dark. "Just as well," he thought. "I'm not ready for a relationship now. Maybe it's better if I don't meet her just yet." But the heart never understands what the mind knows to be true, so he continued to look.

Sitting in his favorite spot on the deck, he scanned the coastline, then eased back against the seat cushions and looked up at the mast of the boat. The acrid smell of marsh filled his nostrils, bringing a smile to his lips. He had always loved the marshes. As a young boy, he loved to dig and play in the mud. He would take off in the morning wearing camouflage shorts and knee-high rain boots. He always took a bucket to bring home his treasures, anything from fiddler crabs to old bottles that the tides had pushed around.

By the time Matthew hit middle school, he would count the days until the weekends or summers when he could spend his days exploring. His parents had bought him a small Jon boat with a trolling motor and instructed him that he had to be able to see his house at all times. Thankfully, his home was one of the largest ones on Isle of Hope, so he could go quite far. During one of his big exploring days in the first week of summer, he met Louey. Matthew had pulled his boat on a small oyster rake and was carefully walking the mud when he noticed a patch of oysters. They were closed and beautiful. *My mom would be so happy if I brought these home for supper,* he thought, and he began trying to pull them apart with his hands. The outer oysters dislodged fairly easily, but the inner ones were attached in clusters. Not knowing much about oysters or how they grew, he used all his might trying to pull them apart, until his grip slipped and the oyster shell dug deep into his hand. He screamed as he looked down at the mingling of mud and blood, searching the shoreline to see his house. But instead, he saw Louey.

Louey's six-foot frame filled his small boat. A scar ran from his mouth across his brown face toward his ear. He had heard the stories of Louey from the kids at school, but the man before him didn't seem intimidating. He wore old khaki pants covered with a year's worth of mud, and his hands and arms were smeared with the same. When he spoke, the scar on his face moved. "Hey there, young fella. Ya need some help?"

Holding up his hand, he answered, "Yes, sir. I think I do."

Louey held up a similar scar on his hand in acknowledgement before answering, "Okay, then. Why don't you hop over here in my boat, and we'll pull yours behind? Where do you live, boy?"

Matthew pointed to his house on the bluff.

"Your daddy, Mr. Mike?"

"Yes, sir."

Louey only nodded and helped Matthew into his boat. He wrapped his hand with a stark white t-shirt that was stored under the seat, told Matthew to hold his hand at eye level to be above his heart, and then quickly covered the distance. When they docked, he told Matthew to walk up to his house and that he would take care of his boat. Matthew only nodded, then looked at the t-shirt which was completely soaked by then, and walked up to his house.

The rest of the day had been a blur of hysterics, beginning the moment he walked into the house. By the end of the day, he had fourteen stitches and was restricted from ever going out on the water alone. The following week was the worst of his life. He would sit on the bluff, watching the boats go in and out, knowing he was alone on the shore.

Until one day, there was a knock on the door. When he answered, Louey was standing on the other side. "Where you been, boy? Ain't them oysters been calling you?"

"Yes, sir, they are. But I'm not allowed out on the water alone anymore."

"Then why don't you come with me?"

"You'd let me do that?"

"Only on one condition."

"What's that?"

"You let me teach you the right way to take the oysters, then you help me whenever you can."

Matthew wanted to hug him right there on the spot, but he awkwardly extended his non-bandaged left hand and said, "You've got yourself a deal."

His mama wasn't thrilled; she had heard talk of Louie, too. But his dad loved the idea. "Instead of wasting my money all summer long, you'll be the only middle schooler bringing home money. I'll even set you up a bank account for a new boat." And true to his word, by the end of the summer, he had saved enough money to buy a small used boat.

Mathew spent every summer and many afternoons after school on the long flat boat, getting out in the mud oystering.

But when he began high school, he found the second love of his life: baseball. His two worlds competed, each holding a piece of his heart, turning and pulling in happy competition until the day the Notre Dame scout came to Benedictine.

"I don't think I can do it," he told his dad. "I'm not as smart as the other guys looking at Notre Dame and...," his voice softened. "And, the only water near South Bend, Indiana, are lakes."

"I understand, son," his father had told him. "But this is a chance of a lifetime."

Matthew had taken that chance, leaving behind the South and his coastal waterways. Yet, he always enjoyed his visits home. Year by year, he noticed the fast changes happening to the water. Restrictions had been implemented so people could not eat seafood caught in specific areas. The hepatitis scare of raw oysters made locals double-check their "R" months, but the Low Country's weather was unpredictable and sometimes much warmer than anticipated. Then, there were the bacteria issues running the length of the Savannah River. It extended to Tybee, where they had to close the beaches some weeks in the middle of the summer.

"Has it always been like this?" he had asked his dad.

"Like what?" came the voice of a man who worked in an office. By the time he got his seafood, it had been perfectly prepared.

When he asked some of his buddies who had stayed in Savannah after high school graduation, they agreed that the pollution in the waterways had worsened. "It's like that up and down the East Coast," they answered. "Man has become greedy in taking and not giving back to the ocean."

That statement saddened Matthew. But what could he do? He was just one man, sitting in Chicago, teaching high school boys how to pitch. But now he was home, and the question resurfaced. *What can I do?*

He closed his eyes, breathing in the smell of fiddler crabs running in the mud. "Man, I love the water," he said into the wind. It was one of the many reasons he chose to be home. He thought about that statement, focusing on the words, "I chose." He chose to come home, he wasn't forced to. But now what? Turning back to the coastline, he decided to move the sailboat into a slip during the weekend and live there until he found another place. *I've spent too much time trying to make my future in baseball. The time has come to figure out how to help the city I love. I need to reconnect with Savannah,* he thought. Then he nodded his head just once to seal the deal.

17

THE OYSTER STEW CREW

Agnes thought she was early until she pulled into the parking lot and found the Oyster Stew Crew already at work. Lottie had told her they came twice a week in the early morning hours to make her recipe of the stew and package it up to be sent across the U.S. "They run like a well-oiled machine," Agnes had been told, but she had not met them until now.

As soon as she opened the door, she was surrounded by the sound of laughter and Reggae music. Everyone was talking and enjoying one another as if they weren't working at all. Agnes stood inside the doorway for the longest time unnoticed and couldn't help but laugh, too. Their accent was from the Caribbean, and they were obviously all family, husbands and wives and most likely a few grown children, too. Everyone had their place. The men had covered the butcher block island in plastic and were shucking the oysters so fast that shells were flying in every direction. The women were chopping, mixing, and stirring while the adult children carried the tubs of finished stew into a cooling section in the refrigerator. Then, there were three older women sitting at the counter, dipping up portions into containers.

We share this kitchen, but they leave it like no one has been here, Agnes thought. The only way she'd known of their presence over the last few weeks was from the smell of oysters and the refrigerator loaded with containers.

Agnes watched a bit longer, but when an obvious favorite song came on, they all began dancing. Somewhere, in the middle of a hip-flinging, wide spin, one of the stirrers locked eyes with Agnes and belted out a scream. "Oh, Lawd! It's a little girl. Look here," she called to the group, who had all stopped working when she had bellowed out.

Agnes shrunk down and waved nervously, "Hi everyone. I'm Agnes. I, well, I own the place."

They looked to one another, quickly wiped their hands, and turned the music off. They gathered around Agnes, welcoming her to the group, each one talking and asking questions at the same time. Finally, the lady who had noticed her first designated herself as the spokesperson and got everyone's attention. Everyone went quiet and waited for her to talk. She then introduced each person in the room by name. When she was done, she turned to Agnes and nodded her head.

"I'm so happy to finally meet all of you. I'm sorry I came in so early this morning and interrupted you. If you need anything from me, please let me know. Please, go back to what you were doing."

The music came back on, and everyone returned to work except for one of the shuckers. He held out his hand and introduced himself again as Gary.

After shaking hands, Gary got right to the point. "Miss Lottie always found the right sources for our oysters for the stew. Sometimes, she would drive long distances to find them. I think it's time to find new oysters again. We just got a new shipment for this batch, and they should be sending their best oysters at this time of year, but they are not plump enough. The recipe calls for plump oysters, which almost pop in your mouth. These are small. They are not what we need."

"Where are these oysters from?"

"They are from Florida. I think the last hurricane might have damaged the beds. We always bought from a place in Canada until a friend of hers asked her to try using local oysters. Maybe we should go back to the original ones."

"Do you happen to know the name of the place in Canada?" Agnes asked, but knowing the answer.

"On Prince Edward Island," he answered. "A town called Cavendish."

Agnes stood behind the counter, looking out over the many tables in the café. It was finally how she wanted it. Although she had kept a diner vibe, it now had a homey feeling that Lottie's never did.

She remembered standing at that same counter when she was in high school. She had watched Lottie meeting with an artist to design the label for her oyster stew. Lottie was so confident in what she was doing. She never apologized for being independent, and she never asked for permission or forgiveness.

"I sure wish I was more like you," Agnes mumbled.

"You are," a small voice whispered in her ear. Or was it a voice she had conjured up from a distant memory? Either way, it made her smile.

The tribe fell silent the moment they spilled through the front door. The sight of Agnes grinning from ear to ear as she looked out over her diner brought all conversation to a stop, which was rare.

"Well, don't you just look like the cat that swallowed the canary," Latrice blurted out.

Agnes seemed surprised they had entered the door without her noticing and quickly moved to welcome them. Their eyes wandered the room as Agnes seated them before darting to the kitchen. They each went around the table, telling their friends about their week and anything exciting that was happening. The six of them were settling back into life in Savannah and were purposefully leaning on each other. Agnes dashed between the kitchen and the table, trying out all the dishes she would be serving at the restaurant. At the end of the meal, Agnes brought out a pot of coffee and a pan of her favorite sticky buns.

"Oh my gosh, Agnes. Where did you get these from?" asked Maggie.

The whole table looked to her for an answer.

"I made them myself. I didn't outsource anything that you ate today."

"Yum," Kathleen grunted in between bites. "I knew you worked here with Lottie while you were at St. Vincent's, but I sure didn't know you could cook so well."

Agnes replied, "Yeah, this may sound crazy, but cooking makes me happy. When I watch others enjoy my dishes, it's a feeling like no other. My friends from Notre Dame think I'm crazy. 'You don't graduate from N.D. and become a cook,' they keep telling me. But I can't imagine living in Chicago working my tail off right now. Lottie knew..." She let the sentence hang in the air until Stephanie finished it.

"Lottie knew what was best."

Agnes smiled, "Yes. She always did."

"Well, you've really got something here, Agnes," Latrice chimed in, gesturing around the room. "And what about the oyster stew business?"

"It has continued to run this whole time, just like a well-oiled machine," Agnes answered, pulling up a chair and plopping down. She poured herself a cup of coffee and leaned into the group. "Do you really think I can do this?"

Stephanie answered first. "Oh yeah. The café is cozy, and the food is to die for. It makes you feel like you're in your mama's kitchen, except my mama never cooked."

They all laughed and agreed.

"So, you're calling it Aggie's?" Jan asked.

"Lottie knew what would become of the restaurant far in advance, and she named it." Agnes swept her hand to gesture across the room, then smiled like she did when they arrived and said, "Welcome to Aggie's."

18

UNCLE CARL

Gladys had finally located Uncle Carl's grave in Greenwich Cemetery. His plot had been easy to find—a little overgrown but looking great. She struggled as she tried to place the flowers where they wouldn't fall over, but on her third grunt, she had anchored them in an old, rusty holder pushed into the ground. Staring at his headstone, she whispered, "I am so grateful to you for saving my life that Fourth of July. Thank you, Uncle Carl."

She shuffled to a stone bench and let her mind wander. It had been doing that more than she wanted to admit since she'd been back in Savannah. This time, she could feel Uncle Carl carrying her to his car. God bless that man. They had driven all night through South Carolina, North Carolina, and into Virginia. As the sun had begun to rise, reality had set in. She would never be returning to Savannah, not only for her own safety but also for the safety of her family.

Uncle Carl took her as far away as he could—Boston. She was to catch the train from there to go to his wife's relatives on Prince Edward Island in Canada.

"Once you're in Charlottetown, get a place for the night, then make your way to Cavendish," he instructed.

She had agreed while picking his brain for every stitch of information he had on the relatives he had only met once.

She could barely hold her eyes open when they finally drove into Boston. Her head felt hot and heavy, and her foot pounded. She knew without a doubt that the cut on her foot was infected.

He pulled into the train station, bought her the ticket, and emptied the rest of the cash from his pockets into her hand. When she began to refuse, telling him that he needed gas to get home, he waved her off.

"I love you like one of my own. It's gonna kill me not telling your family you are safe, but your secret will die with me. God has big plans for you. Go and live your life." The last words were garbled by the cry in his throat. When he kissed her forehead goodbye, he stopped and held her head in his hands. "You're burning up," he whispered.

She nodded. "I'll be fine. I promise. Now go," she said sternly and turned to climb on the train. Settling into a seat, she fell into a deep sleep. She vaguely remembered the train making stops: a young woman in a habit boarded and sat across from her, a family got on and then got off, the train went through a tunnel, and then it boarded a ferry.

She was awakened by the sound of her moans as the train exited the ferry. Her eyes locked with the young woman across from her, who looked at her with sympathy. "I'm studying to be a nurse. Will you let me give you some water?"

Gladys only nodded, but that one nod set the young woman in motion. She took care of Gladys for the rest of the trip.

Charlottetown was the final stop, so they made everyone exit the train. Gladys couldn't move. She vaguely heard the noises around her, but they were blurred as if she were listening from under the water. Had the ferry sunk? She no longer cared. Finally, she felt someone lifting her. She was jostled one way and the other until she felt the cold hit her face. She tried to reason why it would be cold in July, but nothing made sense. The last thing she remembered was her foot on fire. What were they doing to her? Then, she was out.

The sound of birds woke her. Forcing her eyes open, she watched a fan spin overhead. She tried to lift her head, but the weight was too much.

"Hello?" she called out. "Is anyone there?"

An unfamiliar face came into her sight. A nun with the bluest eyes she'd ever seen. "You're awake? We were beginning to worry," she exclaimed.

Gladys' eyes darted around the room. "Where am I?"

"You are in a hospital in Charlottetown."

"Then I made it," Gladys said in an exhale.

"Where are you from?" the nun asked.

"Boston," she said in a half-lie. "I'm going to visit family in Cavendish."

"You're not visiting anywhere for a while. You have a very bad cut on your foot that has caused an infection in your leg. It seems to be healing, but we've been praying we won't have to take your leg to stop the spread. So far, our medicine and prayers seem to be working."

Gladys tried to wiggle her toes and cried out in pain.

"Be still, child. You have a lot of healing ahead. For now, you need your rest."

"Thank you, Sister." Her words trailed off while she struggled to keep her eyes open, but they won. So, she drifted into a deep sleep.

The next time she awoke, it was the middle of the night. Darkness surrounded her bed. The only light in the room was a small metal lamp, illuminating a desk stacked with folders. She felt her stomach growl and laid her hands on her belly to try to quiet it. This time, she was able to lift her head.

Noticing the young novice from the train, she called out to her. "Hey. Hey, you."

The girl put her finger to her lips to shush her and walked in Gladys' direction. "It's the middle of the night. Everyone's asleep."

"I'm sorry," Gladys whispered. "But I'm starving. Can you please get me something to eat?"

The girl smiled and nodded curtly. "That's a good sign. I'll be right back."

She returned with a cold biscuit and a glass of apple juice.

Agnes barely put it in her mouth before she threw up. The smell alone had made her stomach lose its contents. "I'm so sorry. I'm not sure what happened."

The nun smiled. "What kind of nurse would I be if I couldn't see vomit?"

"Thank you for everything, especially for taking care of me on the train. I wouldn't be here without you."

"I just want you to feel better," the girl said in a whisper, then looked around the room to make sure she hadn't disturbed any of the patients.

"One day, I'll repay you. I promise," Gladys said.

Again, the girl only nodded and walked away.

Gladys sat alone in the dark, her future completely unknown. She wiggled her toes, grateful that the pain told her that her foot was still there. The nausea crept up the back of her throat, and she grabbed the bag she was still holding just in time. *What is this all about?* she wondered. She always had an iron stomach. She tried to settle back in. When she closed her eyes this time, she couldn't sleep as thoughts of the past week swirled in her mind. A tear trickled from the corner of her eye and hit the pillow.

She wondered how her family was and wished she could tell them she was safe. Then, as if being summoned, a picture of Lottie flooded her mind. She focused on her image until she could see the color of her lipstick, then murmured softly, "I'm safe, and I love you." At that moment, she understood, without a doubt, that Lottie knew she was alive. But had Lottie known then what she had done?

Gladys' mind became fuzzy as the sound of a passing boat moving along the Wilmington River snapped her back to the present. Greenwich was an addition to Bonaventure Cemetery and shared the same bluff. She glanced at Uncle Carl's headstone one last time before returning to the car.

"This trip may have done more harm than good, especially to me. There are too many bad memories here," Gladys said to herself. "It's about time for me to go home." As soon as she returned to the cottage, she planned the rest of her trip and booked her return flight for two weeks away.

19

YOUTH GROUP

Matthew scanned the gym, looking for Father Sullivan, but only one girl was inside playing basketball. *She's really good,* he thought as he watched her dribble and take a long shot. When it swished in without touching the rim, he began to clap.

She turned so quickly she almost fell to the ground. When their eyes met, his breath caught. "Agnes?" he said, confused. "What are you doing here?" He watched her eyebrows furrow as her eyes darted around the gym, looking for something or someone she didn't see. Then, standing tall, she squared her shoulders and answered.

"Hello, Matthew. Father Sullivan asked me to meet him to talk about the possibility of helping with the youth group this year. It was so important to me in high school, so I told him I'd consider it. What are you doing here?"

Shaking his head, he answered, "He asked me to help, too."

They stood facing one another, but neither spoke. They were soon interrupted by a booming voice. "My two superstars. Thank you for saying you'd help out. I'm assuming the two of you know one another?"

They both mumbled they did, so he began to explain. "Our program has about eighty high schoolers. It's a little different than when you were here. We meet every Sunday afternoon during the school year and then do a service project in the summer. You both have shared with me about your mission trips to Guatemala that changed your life, so I was hoping you could work together to find a good program for us over the summer."

Matthew and Agnes' eyes locked. *Does she remember?* Matthew wondered, then felt the familiar pull in his gut. Was it embarrassment or regret? He never was quite sure. He cleared his throat and answered the kind priest.

"Sounds great, Father. Sign me up."

Father Sullivan beamed, shook Matthew's hand, and then turned his attention to Agnes. Matthew watched as Agnes wrung her hands. Why did her nervousness make him smile? He knew it wasn't his place, but all he wanted to do was protect her, so he pulled the priest's attention away with a question.

"What do you need us to do?"

"Oh, right. Today, just observe. Get to know the other adult leaders and, more importantly, the teens."

The sound of the gym door flying open drew everyone's attention as the mass of teens all seemed to arrive simultaneously.

"All right. I'm off. Have fun, you two," Father Sullivan called over his shoulder, leaving them alone at the top of the three-point line. They didn't have time to talk further as every teenage boy ran onto the court.

Agnes forgot she was holding the ball under her arm until the rowdy boys began teasing her to shoot. So, she dribbled to the right, stopping just outside the three-point-line and put up her favorite shot. When the ball swished through, the young men all "Woo'ed" in unison. Then, one of them challenged her.

"You shoot until you miss."

She nodded in acceptance and clapped her hands for the ball. She then made the ring, stopping at each of the five shooting spots they would take daily in practice. The boy with the big mouth fed the ball back to her after each shot. One after the other, they dropped right in. After four years of those practices, she could do it with her eyes closed. When she finished, she said, "Okay, hot shot. Your turn." But he laughed and declined, saying, "You and I are the captains. Let's choose teams."

The game only lasted fifteen minutes while everyone was arriving, but in those few minutes, she had gotten to know all the teenagers playing with her. They sought her out throughout the rest of the night as they went through testimonies, activities, and praise and worship. And when they left, they told her they couldn't wait to see her next week. Just like that, she was sold.

Matthew was standing beside Father Sullivan when Agnes passed them on her way out of the gym. She smiled at the priest and simply said, "I'm in."

Matthew smiled as he watched her go, but she turned back when she opened the gym door. Her eyes searched until they rested on Matthew. Smiling, she raised her hand goodbye, then the door shut behind her.

"Whoa, I feel some sparks there," Father Sullivan teased.

"Yeah, that's a long-time spark. But with her comes commitment and staying in Savannah."

The priest nodded, "Yes, but isn't that a good thing?"

Matthew rubbed the razor stubble on his chin. "Yes, I guess it is. I don't know." He paused for a second. "You asked us about Guatemala. Did you know we were there together?"

The priest raised his eyebrows. "Ah, the plot thickens."

Matthew nodded and said goodnight, but on the ride home, his thoughts were of Agnes. He should have told her that morning in Guatemala, but he was embarrassed. How do you tell a woman you're discerning the priesthood because your mom asked you to? You don't. But he had listened to his mom. She was sweet and only wanted what was best for him.

She had told him, "When I was younger, every young man discerned the priesthood before choosing their career. They would give six months of themselves and not date during that time, leaning only on the sacraments. After those six months, they would know."

Selfishly, he knew he wasn't dating anyone and thought those six months would help him focus on the last two quarters of school without any female distractions, so he agreed. He talked to his spiritual director and then made a promise to his mom. He hadn't anticipated that Agnes Reed would be on his mission trip.

20

GUATEMALA

On the drive home, Agnes pondered her evening. It had been a fun night, and she had also learned a lot from the program. But would she be able to work with Matthew?

She pulled under the carport of her dark driveway. As she got out of her car, something on the back of the property caught her eye. After letting her eyes adjust to the dark, she realized light was coming from the shed at the back of the property. *There can't be a light on,* she thought. *It must be a reflection of the moon on something inside.* She shrugged it off. When she moved into her aunt's house, she had so many other things to focus on that she had pushed aside anything related to the yard. And in her mind, the shed belonged to the yard. "You'll have to wait," she said into the wind, and walked inside.

After pouring a large glass of wine, she wandered onto the back porch, settled into a comfy chair, and let her mind wander. Her thoughts quickly went to Guatemala, and the memories started flooding in.

Every year, during the first week of summer, Notre Dame offered its athletes the opportunity to go on a mission trip to

Guatemala. Agnes' roommate had talked her into going, but she hadn't taken the time to mentally prepare for it. Her class schedule required her total attention, so the packet titled "Guatemala Mission Trip" was not opened until she was seated on the plane prior to takeoff.

Reading the small brochure, she learned about the Guatemalan people, the civil war that had torn them apart, and the Mayan culture. She also read about the terrain of mountains and volcanos around a country the size of Kentucky. Lastly, she learned about their Catholic faith.

Leaning back into her plane seat, she closed her eyes, trying to picture the faces of the people she would meet in the countryside and small villages. But she wasn't prepared for the crowd of faces in Guatemala City. After a very abrupt landing on an airstrip nestled in the valley between many mountains, the large group drove to their meeting place at a hotel in Guatemala City. Agnes had been stunned as they traveled the streets toward their hotel. Not only were there young children on the streets selling small boxes of bubble gum, but there were also armed military soldiers on every corner, which made her extremely uncomfortable. She was happy when they finally arrived at their hotel.

They freshened up and went to a welcome dinner, where they were broken into groups. As she searched the room for her group, she noticed Matthew. He was sitting with several other volunteers under a sign that read, "Group 4." He smiled as she approached and welcomed her to the group, scooting to offer her a seat next to his.

The leader welcomed them and explained their assignment. They would be traveling to Antiqua, a small town in the mountains of Guatemala, about an hour away, and working in a church that ran an orphanage. Agnes beamed. For the first time since she had left South Bend, she became excited to travel to the small town outside the city.

They left the following morning. Soon after leaving the city, they began to travel down unpopulated roads full of farms, mostly growing coffee beans. The bus bumped round and round every mountain it could find. Agnes knew she was prone to motion sickness and had taken medicine before leaving the hotel, but no medicine known to man could combat the mountains around Guatemala.

Matthew noticed she had stopped conversing with the group and had asked if she was all right. She explained that she easily got car sick, so he asked the students in the van to reposition her so she could move to the front seat. But that wasn't enough. The small roads on the mountainside didn't allow room to pull over, so she had to hang her head out the window of the old van as it continued to move along. Every time her head thrust out the window, the passengers would groan in response. And every time Agnes pulled herself back inside, she would apologize to the group.

She had never been so happy to arrive anywhere and contemplated never again leaving the orphanage. The group nicknamed her "Hurl," which she wasn't proud of, but at least it brought humor to an awful situation.

As everyone began to pile out of the old van, Agnes took in large gulps of the clean mountain air and felt her stomach ease. A girl named Hailey offered her a tissue and stood near her sympathetically. Matthew began passing out the luggage, calling each bag's owner. "Hailey," he announced, tossing the bag out. "Hurly," he then called. Making eye contact with Agnes, he winked. She apologized one last time as she retrieved her bag and was rewarded with everyone patting her back on her return.

The sisters inside the orphanage greeted the group with broken English until one of them narrowed in on Agnes and began speaking to her in rapid Spanish. At first, she was embarrassed; they assumed she could speak Spanish because she was

Hispanic. However, being raised in America, she only knew Spanish from two years at SVA. She was literally the only one in the tribe who couldn't roll her R's.

Agnes reversed the situation for a moment. If a group of Guatemalan students came to America with one Anglo in the group, naturally, most Americans would direct their conversation to the Anglo. So why would this be different? Still, she was relieved when her group leader intervened and got directions for the week ahead.

While Matthew and two others were working to deepen and purify the orphanage's well, the rest of the group was helping the kind sisters who ran the orphanage while working with the children with dark brown eyes. Agnes felt a connection to them, a connection that no one in her group knew. She, too, didn't have her birth mom present in her life. And for the first time, she viewed adoption as the beautiful gift that it was, the gift of unconditional love.

She and Matthew had been inseparable during their free time that week. They were drawn to one another. In the afternoons, the group could wander around the city and enjoy the local cuisine and coffee, wandering in the cute shops and little cafes. She still had the picture of the group standing in front of the Santa Cataline Arch on her refrigerator.

They were given their last day in Antiqua off. It had been a long week, and the rest of the group wanted to sleep late, but Agnes and Matthew both got up early to hike to the top of Cerro de la Cruz, which means the Hill of the Cross.

It was a steady climb, but after thirty minutes, they reached the top and carefully sat on the edge of the surrounding wall. Dangling their feet over the edge, they sat silently, enjoying the panoramic view of Antigua. It was Agnes who broke the silence.

"Could this be any more perfect?" she asked, looking across the horizon.

She felt Matthew's stare and turned toward him. His eyes had locked with hers. She was sure he was about to kiss her, so she eased toward him ever so slightly. However, he pulled back in response.

"I'm so sorry, Agnes, if I misled you. Please forgive me," he said, jumping to his feet.

But once again, something had scared him, and that something had been more powerful than his pull toward her.

Agnes' face still burned thinking about that moment, or maybe it was the wine. Letting her eyes scan the dark marsh, she noticed the absence of the lonely sailboat for the first time and somehow missed its presence. She had already committed to working with the youth group, but she made a pact with herself to protect her heart, and the one person it needed protection from was Matthew Monroe.

21

THE SHED

The rattling of dishes from the kitchen got her attention. She had been deep in thought, sitting in the living room attempting to write a business plan for Aggie's. But as the sound grew louder, she swore she heard horses. Tossing her pen on the coffee table, she quickly walked toward the porch. Nature always responds to natural events, and she wondered if Savannah could be having a small earthquake. Or, by the amount of rattling, it could be as big as the great quake of 1886. Yet when she opened the porch door, she was met with the sounds of a normal day, birds chirping, and the sound of a leaf blower in the distance.

What is going on with this house? she wondered, and not for the first time. There were many "unexplainables" that came with the property, things that made her very uncomfortable. "This might have been Lottie's thing, but it surely isn't mine," she muttered.

It wasn't the first time she thought she had heard horses. The sounds of "neighing" had woken her in the middle of the night the week prior. And then there were the strange feelings when walking in the backyard behind the shed, almost as if a large something was walking beside her. She knew there had to be answers but had no idea who to even ask.

The shed was something she had put off since the night she had seen the light. She had covered every inch of the house, even the attic. Lottie had purged everything. If it wasn't something she used daily, she had gotten rid of it. Every closet, every dresser, every cabinet held only the essentials. It was strange how someone could just walk away from life. But what about the shed? Maybe it held all of the answers to her many questions.

I guess this day is as good as any, she thought. So she went through her keys, pulled out the one that read "Shed," and walked toward the back of the yard. She had the strangest feeling she was being watched and glanced toward the border of the property. She was met by only the sway of the expansive azaleas planted decades before. Turning her focus to the shed, she continued walking.

The shed itself was made of brick, Savannah Gray, to be exact. Vines covered most of it, but they seemed to have been planted purposefully, almost as if to camouflage the small building. It was much larger than it appeared from the main house, making her wonder if it was a shed at all. Her curiosity made her excited to find out what was inside.

She narrowed her gaze to where she had seen the light. As she approached, she slowly reached her hands into that hole. Pulling the vines back, she found a full window beneath. The vines had covered all but one of its panes. The window was far too dirty to see inside, so she slowly made her way around. She found two more windows on the side of the shed closest to the main house but no door. *Strange. Who would build a cottage with no door to the bluff?* She wondered, only to realize that nothing had been normal since the day she moved in.

She walked slowly around the outside, passed the side wall with no windows and then turned the corner to the front. This side had a door that had not only been maintained; it had been manicured. To its left was a large swinging barn-like door which also appeared to be in working order. She stood still before it but could not make herself go inside.

Taking a deep breath, she pushed the unlocked door open. "Well, I'll be," she said as her eyes adjusted to the cute office. She let her eyes wander slowly. There were tons of books on shelves and propped in stacks wherever there was room. A comfy chair sat in the corner with a worn quilt spread across its back, and a reading light sat on a small table beside it. There was a desk with writing paper, ready for someone to begin a letter. Lastly, there was a prayer corner with a crucifix, a stack of funeral cards, rosary beads, and various-sized candles placed neatly on the table.

Light spilled through the windows on the door side and somehow showed through the expanse of vines in the back. Beige and white throw pillows and faded quilts were scattered around, making the room cozy. For the first time since moving to this property, Agnes could picture her aunt in this space. "Oh, Lottie. It's beautiful here." She slowly ran her finger along the back of the chair, happy to have found her new favorite spot in Savannah.

Glancing along the side wall with no windows, she noticed three doors. *This must be where Lottie hid all her stuff.* Sure enough, closet one was packed full of things she would need to return and go through. Closet two was full of books, with a set of small books that looked like journals tied up with a blue ribbon. *This looks like the same ribbon from my box*, she thought, making a mental note to come back and look through them. Nothing prepared her for what she would find when she opened the third closet door—downward stairs. The remains of a fake panel of sorts had been pushed to the side to expose stairs that had once been hidden.

In Coastal Georgia, you never found stairs that went underground. The water table was too high. Most swimming pools had to be built up to have a deep end. And even then, sometimes they were only six feet. So, underground stairs in Savannah were unheard of. Unless.

Agnes thought for a moment. Unless the ground was a high bluff, like at The Pirates House downtown. She had never considered Isle of Hope a high point, but the stairs told otherwise. She looked inside. "Creepy, creepy dungeon stairs," she said as she flipped on a light switch inside. A cold iron rail led her down the brick stairs made from the same bricks as those on the cottage's exterior. She was overtaken by the smell of dirt, musty and wet. She descended eight steps before the staircase hit a small landing and turned back directly under the cottage. Pausing, she wondered if she should continue. "Oh, what the hell. I've come this far," she whispered and walked into a simple dirt-floored room where the ceiling was the same floor as the cottage.

The room was no accident. She wondered if it was built at the same time as the cottage. And what was it built for? Would it be a root cellar?

She took one step inside, but something spooked her. She stood very still and could almost hear singing somewhere far off in the distance. She quickly turned and began to run up the stairs when the floor above began to shake. She stopped. This time, there was no doubt; it was the sound of horses, and they were running on her property. She flew up the stairs and burst out the cottage door. Frantically, she ran to the back of the yard, but there was nothing. How could there be nothing? She knew what she heard; she had been hearing it for weeks. Walking until the grass gradually morphed into the marsh, she stopped when her shoes began to sink.

The sound of movement behind her made her spin around. The smell of earth and leather hit her in the face. This time, she closed her eyes and pictured a tall brown mare, skittish in her presence. "Whoa there," she said softly, extending her hand. She was shocked when she felt a hot breath on her fingers, followed by the wetness of an animal's nose. She awkwardly whispered into the breeze, "Good girl," then her eyes flew open to nothingness while the prickle of hair on her arms convinced her otherwise.

22

THE MYSTIC

T*his property holds so many secrets. Could there possibly be more?* she wondered as she made her way back to the house. She was scared that the answer might be "yes."

Something made her glance down Mystic Lane, and she was surprised to see Matthew standing at the end of her driveway. He seemed stunned to see her and awkwardly began to call out something to her that she couldn't understand.

"That damn B.C. mumble," she said under her breath, knowing that most men who attended Benedictine Military School mumbled. Attending four years of an all-male school gave them the privilege of grunting and growling at each other and still being understood. Agnes simply shook her head and raised one hand toward her ear, indicating she couldn't hear him.

Matthew walked down her driveway. Once he was closer, he tried again. "You live here?"

"Yes, I do."

Running his hand through his hair, he looked past her in confusion. "Do you have a roommate?" Matthew asked.

"No," she responded, losing her patience. "Why do you ask?"

He stammered, kicking the gravel drive with his shoe, then squared her gaze. "Do you like to dance?"

Like to dance? What is he talking about? Then, it hit her, causing her eyes to widen with fear. The corners of his mouth raised into a small smile, which infuriated her. "Have you been watching me?" she spit out angrily.

"No," he answered quickly, then changed his answer. "Well, not really." Meeting her eyes, he admitted. "Well, yes. But not on purpose."

Her face burned like she had been slapped. "Explain. NOW!" she demanded, swallowing down the lump in her throat.

"As you know, I moved back home."

"Yeah. And?"

"And I didn't want to move back in with my family. So, they let me moor the sailboat and live on the water. And the other night, I was sitting on the deck, drinking a beer and minding my own business, when..."

"Stop!" she cut him off. "I've heard enough. Goodbye, Matthew." Agnes turned toward the house and began walking away.

"Wait," he called out, following on her heels.

She continued walking, but he was quickly by her side.

"I don't mean to embarrass you. Come on, Agnes."

Agnes slowed to a stop, ready to give him a piece of her mind, but was surprised to find him scanning his surroundings. The look on his face was that of a child in wonder. She watched him but didn't say a word.

"I've never been on The Mystic before," he uttered as his eyes moved upward toward the mist encircling the trees.

"The Mystic?" Agnes asked, quickly forgetting she was angry with him. There was no awkwardness or discomfort as before. They searched each other's eyes, hoping to somehow read the other's mind. She was surprised to feel his hand touch hers.

"Can we talk for a bit?" Matthew asked calmly.

Agnes looked down at her watch but wasn't sure why. As much as she wanted to go and hide under her bed in embarrassment, she wanted answers even more. With a forced smile, she agreed and asked him into the house.

She walked him around the side and onto the porch, then motioned for him to sit in one of the chairs against the house facing the water. She was surprised when he went in the opposite direction and sat in Lottie's chair. *Of all the chairs on the porch, he went to that one?* As always, she found her way to the glider.

"Tell me about The Mystic," she began.

"I can only tell you what's been told to me over the years, passed down through my family. I have no idea if any of it is fact or fiction," he answered.

"I understand. But I'd still love to hear," she replied.

"Okay then." Matthew cleared his throat and began. "The land is called 'The Mystic,' but no one is sure why. The area has always appeared to have a low-lying fog hovering above it, even on sunny days. The constant haze overshadows the property. My granddad said that he was told that the City of Savannah received a request from someone to purchase the land sometime before the Civil War. They were more than happy to take whatever offer was made. Who in their right mind would buy a piece of property that seemed to be surrounded by doom? Next thing you know, a veterinarian built a small house and stable and brought in horses. I hear there were nearly thirty horses roaming around back here. I'm unsure when people started saying the place was haunted, although I do see why they felt that way. As kids, we were terrified of this property, which was confusing because of the nice lady who lived here."

"That was my aunt Lottie," Agnes added.

"Was?" he questioned. And when she nodded, he added. "I'm sorry. I ran into her sometimes at Mass. She always called me by name and patted my head, even when I became much taller than her." He smiled at the thought of the petite woman reaching up and how he would bend over to meet her hand. "Anyway, I really don't know anything more than that." He turned towards Agnes, who intently listened as she stared at the river.

Feeling the weight of his stare, she turned to meet his eyes. "Thank you, Matthew," she said, rising to her feet. She remembered this feeling with him when they shared personal moments like in Guatemala. The butterflies in her stomach indicated she had to get away from him. He had hurt her before, twice, and she had never completely recovered. She blurted out, "I'm gonna run inside and get us some lemonade. I'll be right back," and she bolted from the porch.

Walking into the kitchen, she took down two glasses before the light over the sink came on as if acknowledging who the second glass was for.

"Come on, Lottie. Not him," Agnes mumbled while reaching to turn the light off. She switched it down, then up and down again, but the light stayed on. "Just stay on for all I care," she said aloud and finished pouring the lemonade. Standing at the kitchen door, she took a deep breath. *I can do this. I can handle my emotions.* But when she opened the screen door, she found Matthew looking out over the marsh to where his boat sat, and her heart sank to her stomach. He was so handsome, standing there in his khakis and snug long-sleeve t-shirt. For as long as she could remember, Matthew had turned her to mush. But he had pushed her aside too many times. She could not leave herself open to rejection again.

He turned when he heard the screen door slam, took the lemonade from her, and said thank you. The electric tension bouncing between them made her breath catch. Did he feel it, too? Finally, he began. "It feels odd to be standing on this porch looking out to the spot where my boat sat. I know you're embarrassed, but I want you to know something. Moving home's been hard, but the day I saw you gave me hope. You danced without a care in the world. There's a phrase for that; let me think."

"Dance like no one's watching?" Agnes blurted out.

"Yeah, that's it," Matthew replied.

"But the thing is, someone was watching," Agnes said, shaking her head.

"Yes, but you didn't know. And that person dancing was the real you. It was the first time I felt I was meant to be in Savannah. And to be honest, I've been walking by this house for a month now, hoping to catch a glimpse of the woman I saw dancing on the porch. I was surprised it was you." She shot him a look, and he quickly added, "Pleasantly surprised but surprised just the same." Matthew paused to collect his thoughts, then continued. "You captivated me, and I can't stop thinking about you." He locked eyes with her and didn't turn away.

She was surprised by her thoughts. *I captivated him? What about all those other times he pushed me away? He likes that silent, mysterious person from the porch, not me.* She opened her mouth to speak; at the same moment, he leaned in to kiss her.

"Whoa there!" she said, placing her hand on his chest.

He backed away, but her hand remained.

The look on his face was full of confusion.

"What did I miss?" she asked.

He glanced at her hand, still on his chest, and placed his hand on top of hers. "Don't you feel it, Agnes? This connection? It's always been there with us."

She nodded in agreement, then slowly removed her hand from his chest. "Yes, there is a spark. And yes, I've always felt it. But you've had so many opportunities to be with me and pushed me away. And as much as I want to jump in your arms right now, I still picture myself standing on a mountain in Guatemala, wondering what I did wrong."

He listened intently and said, "I'm sorry if I hurt you. But I promise I'll make it up to you if you allow me to." The wind from the marsh caused her hair to blow into her eyes, and he reached up and pushed it behind her ear. Smiling, he backed away. "Would you like to go out in the boat with me one day next week?"

She wanted to scream 'YES,' but as usual, hid her emotions. Finally, she softly answered, "Sure."

His sideways grin made her stomach flutter. "Great. I'll call you and set up a day." Then he sheepishly added, "I got your number from Father Sullivan."

She pulled back in surprise, which made him laugh. Then he turned and left the same way he had come, down the side of the house.

Picking up the empty glasses, she walked back inside. When she heard the screen door bang behind her, she blew out a breath of relief. *What just happened? Am I really going on a date with Matthew?* Then, with a smile, she muttered what he had said. "He can't stop thinking about me? Well, that's good. Now he knows how that feels."

23

STAIRS OF DEATH

Walking into The Warehouse, the tribe scanned the crowd for an empty table. Every year, in the middle of October, the owners of the abandoned building throw the largest Halloween party of the year, called Fright Night. It was no surprise that it was held in the most haunted building on the Riverfront. People never wondered why it sat empty the rest of the year. The ghosts had scared away many business owners who didn't believe in spirits when they signed the initial contracts but quickly changed their minds once they moved in.

Agnes let her eyes roam around the beamed ceiling, focusing on the many open patches straight up to the sky. "How did they even get a permit for this many people to be here?" she asked the group.

"Don't know, but they did. I saw it stapled to the front door," Latrice answered. "I guess we aren't the only ones to wonder, so they felt compelled to staple it to the entryway."

Stephanie jumped in, "It really is shocking they got a permit. This warehouse was one of the first built on the river to stock cotton that was being shipped out on the skimmers. I actually used it as an example in one of my papers in college about building materials in the 1800s. There was a fire inside that took out this whole level, leaving only the brick. The men who worked as laborers loading and unloading the ships had all been asleep. The wood flooring went up so fast that they had been trapped inside. The write-up in the *Savannah Georgian* said it claimed the lives of several men, a couple of them young boys. But the company re-built quickly, and that's where we're standing right now."

"Good gosh!" Kathleen exclaimed with a shiver. "That's why it gives me the creeps."

"All right, ladies. Don't be Debbie Downers. Let's stop gawking and find the bar," Jan added.

They shimmied through the crowd of costumes, all bouncing to the beat of the live band, until everyone had a drink in hand. Then, they settled at a high-top table near a window looking over River Street.

"I never like the way people act when they're in costume. It's almost like when they're dressed up, they are unaccountable for their actions," Maggie stated.

"I know. See that clown over there?" They all turned toward a smiling clown mask with a cigarette hanging from its mouth. "He pinched my butt."

Latrice looked the clown up and down. "Judging from the tight jeans and pumps, I think your clown is a chick."

Maggie was unaffected, "Oh well, at least that would explain the high-pitched voice."

They all laughed together until Jan held her glass up. "Cheers, ladies!" They all responded with a clinking of glasses.

Agnes swirled the green liquid in her clear plastic party glass. "These are good this year. I was worried when I ordered Witch's Brew, but I like the tart melon flavor. What are you drinking?" she asked Stephanie.

"The Zombie. It tastes exactly like Jack's specialty, Bahama Mama."

"Jack always said he feels like a zombie the next day, so that's pretty fitting," Kathleen added.

Maggie held up her beer. "Does anyone ever *really* know what's in those drinks? I'll stick with something I can open myself. Besides, those sweet drinks give me a headache the next morning."

"Cheers to another year of Fright Night," Latrice announced, but the room went black as she finished her sentence.

Silence fell upon the crowded room. The only light was from the windows overlooking the river. Thankful to have a table beside one of them, the ladies could see each other's faces. They all turned to Kathleen.

A man shouted in the background for everyone to stay calm as they tried to regain the power, but Kathleen shook her head. "That power's not coming back on. We need to get out of here." Her voice scared the others, but she had their full attention. She pointed to a side door and said, "We are slowly going to walk to that door. It leads back to Factor's Walk."

"How do you know?" asked Jan.

"Jack and I snuck out there last year to talk," she answered.

"That's what they're calling it these days. Talking?" Maggie teased.

"Haha. Now listen. We are going to stay together and move slowly along the wall. Keep one hand on the person in front of you at all times until we reach the door. You ready?" Kathleen asked.

Each answered, "Yes," in small voices except for Jan, who picked up her drink first and then called out like an Army officer, "I'm ready!"

"Put your damn drink down, Jan," Stephanie ordered.

"I paid seven dollars for this thing," Jan argued.

"Do you want to be stuck in this building all night with the ghosts of several men?"

"Well, that depends on what they look like."

"Jan!" they all yelled.

She turned up her drink in one gulp and said, "There. I'm ready."

Kathleen added, "Oh. One last thing. Listen, it's important. There's about a twenty-foot drop on the other side of that door. So, look alive when you go through and stay close to the building. You'll be fine there."

"Oh, hell no. You know I'm afraid of heights," Latrice called out.

"You'll be fine," Kathleen said in her calm voice.

They moved away from the window slowly, letting their eyes adjust to the blackness. Feeling their way along the wall, they moved at a snail's pace, trying to advance while still grasping hold of their friend behind them. As they groped toward the complete darkness of the corner, they could hear the panic in the room behind them as the room grew hotter by the minute. A booming male voice asked people to stay calm and stay in their place, but the tribe continued to move. When they finally made it to the door, it was stuck.

"These old doors get warped over time. They just need a good push," Stephanie told the group as they each took a turn pushing until it finally gave way. Instantly, the October night air cooled their faces, and the glow from a nearby streetlight lit that area of the room.

Kathleen pointed to the two-foot-wide stone stoop that led to the small stairway with no rail. The twenty-foot drop to Factor's Walk was terrifying, but the stone stairway appeared sturdy and safe.

Kathleen held onto the door and stepped aside, sending the tribe down the stairs one by one. But almost immediately, people began to follow, pushing their way through the crowd to safety. Kathleen managed to get all her friends down the stairs except for Agnes, trapped on the other side of the swinging door.

"I don't like this," Latrice said as they finally hit Factor's Walk. "They could just knock her right off that stoop." Everyone agreed while slowly making their way directly under where Agnes was above. They heard Agnes warning people about the drop and to stay near the wall, but the tribe knew her well and could see the panic on her face. She was helpless against the rush of people.

As always, Stephanie saw things differently and called out to Agnes. "You are safe. Hold on to that door for balance. It's not going anywhere. Okay?"

Agnes nodded, holding on to the door's handle for dear life while warning the escapees of the drop. As each person walked down the stairs, they accumulated with the tribe on Factor's Walk, watching Agnes help people one by one. As the last person walked down the stairs, one of the bystanders wearing a *Friday the 13th* Jason mask ran back up. Holding his hand out to Agnes, he offered to help her down the stairs.

"Thank you," she said in an unsteady voice when she finally made it to level ground. Her breath caught when he took off his mask. Matthew's smile beamed under the glow of the streetlights. The crowd of people who had been waiting below began to thank Agnes for helping them. She nodded to each of them in acknowledgment, but her attention turned back to Matthew. She noticed she was still holding his hand, and he squeezed a little tighter in response.

"You are amazing, do you know that? You helped every one of these people get out the door safely."

"Then you helped me down safely. Thank you for coming for me."

The tribe interrupted, encircling her with relief. She turned back to Matthew, but her eyes focused on something behind him.

He turned to the large sign that read, "Stairs of Death." It had been posted on the rails leading down from Bay Street to River Street. When she pointed to it, all heads turned.

"Not tonight," she yelled triumphantly. "No sir, not tonight!" And everybody cheered along.

24

INTRODUCTIONS

Agnes' parents asked her over for breakfast the following Tuesday morning. She thought it was odd, being a weekday, but she had been trying to find her place in their lives since she had returned from school. She had kept them at arm's length, trying to stand on her own two feet, but she loved to drop in when she wanted to see them. Her last drop-in had found them in the middle of watching a show they didn't want to pause. Instead, they made her watch the hour-long show with them.

"It could have been worse," she had told the tribe at lunch that Wednesday. "I could have walked in on them naked."

The table had all laughed before Jan said, "They don't do that anymore."

"Well, of course they do," Kathleen explained. "My parents flirt with each other constantly."

"Don't we want them to still have a good relationship?" Agnes asked.

"Absolutely," Maggie agreed. "But I sure don't want to see it."

Agnes remembered that statement as she approached the

kitchen door. For the first time ever, she wondered if she should knock before barreling in like she always had. Finally, she cracked it and yelled out, "Is anybody home?" knowing full well that they were.

"We're in the kitchen, Agnes. Come on in," her mom called out in response.

She was excited to see them, but as she turned into the kitchen, she was surprised to see they had a guest.

"Hi, Gladys," Agnes said with a nod before kissing her mom on the cheek. "Hey, Mama," she added, then made her way around the table. "Hey, Pops," she told her dad, planting a small kiss on his temple.

Her dad reached up to her playfully and pinched her cheek. "Hey there, Aggie A," he called out in his familiar way, which always made her smile.

She walked to the counter and poured herself a cup of coffee, but when she turned around, all eyes were on her—worried eyes that made her want to run. She looked at her mom and asked, "What's the matter?"

Her mom jumped to her feet and walked over to Agnes. "Not one thing is wrong, but we want to talk to you about something." She forced a meek smile and ran her hand down the side of Agnes' face. "We've got some news—some very exciting news. Come have a seat."

Wearily, Agnes sat at the table. She didn't realize she was still holding the cup of coffee in mid-air instead of setting it on the table until the heat on her fingers began to burn. Setting it down, she said, "Okay, guys. You're scaring me. Out with it."

Her dad began to explain. "Gladys has told you she's Lottie's sister." Agnes nodded, and her dad cleared his throat. "Gladys is also your grandmother."

Agnes let the words settle in her mind. Since she and her siblings were all adopted, their family had prayed for their birth mother or birth parents several times, but birth grand-parent put a whole new spin on everything. Turning to Gladys, she said, "You're gonna need to explain this further."

"My son, Alex, and his beautiful wife were your parents. They were crazy in love with one another and were over the moon when they had you. You should have seen them," her voice cracked as she slid her napkin from the table and into her hand to wipe her eyes.

"You're speaking in past tense. Why?" Agnes asked.

"They both passed away when you were an infant." Gladys began to cry and didn't try to hide it. She was surprised when Agnes took her hand into her own.

"I'm sorry," Agnes whispered.

Gladys' head dropped in despair as she mumbled, "Me, too."

Agnes' mom grabbed her other hand under the table and squeezed it so hard that she felt her bones crack. When Agnes looked at her mom, she was crying, too.

"We didn't know," Agnes' mom said. "Lottie never told us. When she brought you to us, she explained, 'This baby needs a home. I'll get the paperwork together for you.' We were young parents with a house full of boys, and we had never even thought about it. We simply said, 'Yes!'" She raised Agnes' hand to her lips and kissed it softly.

Agnes could read the worry in her mother's eyes. "I love you, Mom. I'm okay. Really." Her mom squeezed her hand one more time before letting go.

Turning to Gladys, Agnes said, "I have so many questions."

"How could you not," she responded.

"I'd like to start from the beginning if you have the time."

Gladys laughed. "Yes. I believe I have the time. I want you to know everything."

Gladys told them about her summer job at General Oglethorpe Hotel, witnessing the triple murder, fleeing to Prince Edward Island, Canada, and starting a new life in

Cavendish where she started her family. Then she told them about Lottie.

"Lottie was the only person to know I was alive. She knew I was alive the moment I woke up in the hospital on PEI. I'm sure you're aware of how she always knew things." They all nodded. "Well, she said she didn't know where I was, but she knew I was safe, and that was good enough for her. She also told my parents and my sister, Lizzie, a few weeks after my funeral. That sounds odd, I know. Anyway, they knew of Lottie's abilities, so they believed her. They each continued to fake their grief for me because they knew the thugs were watching for me.

It wasn't until after my son's funeral that Lottie showed up at my door. She said she had pictured me crossing under the famous metal arched sign in Charlottetown that read "Victoria Row." She said I was crying and holding a screaming baby. I remember that moment. I had just left the lawyer's office, finalizing my custody of you, and I was at the end of my rope. I was grieving for my son and daughter-in-law while taking care of my husband, who was ill. You were screaming at the top of your lungs, and boy, could you scream. I just stood there and cried. I knew how unfair it was for you not to have the family you deserved.

Lottie came looking for me. She begged me to come home. She told me about our niece, who loved children and who had adopted several." She looked at Ruth and smiled. "My sister Lizzie was blessed to have such a remarkable daughter." Gladys touched her fingers to her lips and blew it to her niece.

She sat back in her chair. "I don't remember the last time I talked so much. I might need to lie down for a bit. Could you please run me home?"

Agnes agreed. After helping Gladys into her car, she walked to the driver's side. When she opened the door, she realized Gladys was already snoring.

25

JUST YOU, ME AND THE SEA

Agnes and Matthew had chosen an afternoon the following week to go out in the boat. She had spent almost an hour trying to pick out the perfect outfit, finally putting on a pair of jeans and a windbreaker.

Matthew was walking his gear over to the small trawler when he noticed her in the distance. She slowed when he waved to her, then picked up her pace to close their distance.

"Hey, stalker," she announced when she got within earshot.

He turned and looked behind him as if she had been speaking to someone else. Then, he pointed to himself in question.

"Hey, I call it like I see it," she answered.

"You really can't blame a bloke for watching a beautiful woman."

Her face reddened. "I don't blame you. It's just embarrassing, that's all."

"Embarrassing? I only wish I could move like that," he replied.

"Yeah, okay."

"No, really. Watch." He began to snap his fingers and sway

back and forth, stiff as a board. An older couple walking their dog laughed as they passed, making Agnes giggle, too. "Maybe you could teach me sometime?" he asked.

"Yes, please teach him," the older lady called out before her dog began to pull her towards a passing squirrel.

"Come on," Matthew said, leading the way to the dock. "We only have a couple of hours before the sun goes down. The marsh is so pretty in the October setting sun; you're gonna love it."

Agnes smiled at the thought. She had never lived right on the water before. But since moving into Lottie's house, she had been watching how the marsh turned from green in the summer to gold in the fall. She couldn't wait to see it from a boat.

Matthew felt the tug on his heart when she smiled; it physically shook him. But why? He had known her his whole life. She was his friend's kid sister. He remembered everything about her and could still remember what she looked like with braces in middle school. He remembered being at their house when her date picked her up for prom. And he remembered kissing her gently on the lips on a cold night at the Grotto at Notre Dame. How could he remember everything? And how had every memory now been replaced with uncertainty, protectiveness, and fear: three emotions he only felt when he was with her?

He reached out his hand to her to step over onto the gangway, and then they walked down to the sailboat at the end. Climbing onboard, they crossed to the other side and climbed down to the small skiff. Matthew held his hand out to her in support and led her to the front bench seat. As she settled in, she watched him busy himself putting everything into place, just like he had done hundreds of times before. His movements were practiced and fluid, almost like a dance. She couldn't tear her eyes away but wasn't self-conscious at all. She simply watched him. And in that moment, she understood how he had watched her. Matthew was doing a dance in his own way, and she was shamelessly watching. Was she really that different from him?

She had been so deep in thought that she jumped when he cranked the engine and shoved off. They rode slowly along the bluff, but he pointed up as soon as they came to her house.

She felt so proud to be the owner of such a cute cottage. But what she noticed for the first time was how the inlet turned into a cove that made Agnes' land come to a point. He noticed her focus and cut the engine. She immediately asked, "Does that area keep water? I thought it was only marshland."

"There's marsh closer to the bank, but the bay keeps water. It's also the best oyster rake around."

This information piqued her curiosity. "Oysters? Like you can actually eat them?"

"Heck yeah. They taste amazing from this bay. Different from other oysters around Savannah."

"You've eaten them?" she asked.

Tentatively, he answered, "Yes. I've always loved the waterways and playing in the mud. Once I found out these were just down the creek, I would hop in my little trolling boat and come and grab some for my mom to cook for dinner."

"Hmmm. I wonder if Lottie knew they were back here? She was known for her oyster stew at the restaurant."

"Yes. She caught me back here a couple of times. She walked out to the point every morning, and when she did, she would see me. She'd yell for me to be safe since I was alone but never told me to leave."

"Lottie walked to the point every morning?"

"She sure did. She would just stand there, looking out in every direction over the river, bay, and wetlands."

"I wonder what she was looking for?" she asked.

"I've got a theory on that. But this is your family; you would know better."

"I'd really like to hear your theory," Agnes replied.

"Okay then. People claim your aunt could talk to ghosts. You know that, right?" Agnes nodded. "Well, not only was she watching, she seemed to be listening. Most of the time, she turned her head like when you're trying to hear something far away. She would also nod in response. So, I think she was being called to the sea. By whom, I would have no idea. But I can tell you, when she would see me, her face would change to connect to the present."

Agnes didn't utter a word. Her silence worried Matthew. Should he have kept his mouth shut? Finally, she uttered, "I wonder what she was watching for?" Locking eyes with him, she changed her tone, "Or maybe she was watching for oyster robbers like you."

He laughed. "Yeah, you're probably right."

She pointed to the bay and asked, "Hey, can anyone take oysters from this area, or does it belong to me?"

"Your land is special. You own the right to the oysters down to the low water mark on the river side. In this bay area, you own the rights to all the oysters."

Agnes' face changed as she processed what he had just told her. "So, you were trespassing?"

Matthew held up his hands in mock surrender. "Yes, ma'am. I believe I was," he said with his Southern drawl.

She smiled at the twang in his voice, which wasn't normally there.

"You have the perfect location for an oyster farm," Matthew explained.

She nodded one last time as she looked over the waterways around her property.

"Let's get moving," he announced. "There's much to be seen." They continued along the Skidaway River until it opened into the Wilmington River. The boat seemed to set its course directly into the setting sun. The reflection bouncing off the water blinded her, so she squinted and covered her eyes with her hand.

As the boat slowed, Matthew turned the engine off. "Agnes, look this way," he said. She turned to face the opposite direction, away from the sun, and was stunned by the view. The golden marsh seemed to glow. The last rays of the day shone brightly on the October marsh grass, dancing against the darkening sky.

"I've always loved to watch the colors fill the sky when the sun sets, but I've never looked in the opposite direction. It's beautiful," she said softly.

Matthew walked to the front of the boat and sat down beside her, looking back over the marsh. "This is my favorite time of year on the water. The marsh turns gold, and the fish are biting." He spread his arms behind himself for support and enjoyed the view. They sat side by side, but neither said a word. Agnes scooted closer into the space between them. It was only the smallest movement, but it was the most monumental in his world. It was a moment when his world stood still, and he could picture her scooting closer to him for the rest of his life. At that moment, Matthew knew he was in love with Agnes Reed.

26

GOODBYE, GLADYS

Gladys walked slowly along the bluff, pondering how much more she was going to reveal to Agnes. She had told her most of the story, which would have to be good enough. She didn't want any ties that would bind her to Ron Graci. It was better not to mention him at all.

Agnes appeared to be waiting for her on the front porch as if she knew she was coming. Gladys slowed, wondering if Lottie was right, then shook it off as a coincidence.

Agnes gave her a long hug and then showed her through the house. Glady took the time to look at the trinkets on the table and acknowledge the photographs. Stopping at Lottie and Benjamin's wedding photo, she said, "I saw the date of Ben's passing on his tombstone at Lottie's funeral. What did he die of?"

"Cancer," Agnes answered. "It was really bad at the end."

Gladys nodded at the photograph and then moved to the next room. "This place suits you," she said.

"Yeah, it's beginning to grow on me," Agnes said, suddenly feeling awkward. They hadn't spoken since she found out

Gladys was her grandmother. She had so many questions, but suddenly, not one came to mind.

Once they both were sitting in the living room, Gladys asked, "What do you think of the slave hiding spot?"

"I thought that's what it was," Agnes answered excitedly.

"Lottie told me that Benjamin's grandfather had taken runaway slaves to an island off the coast for safety. But sometimes they had to wait until they knew it was safe to travel."

Agnes nodded, thinking of the sounds she had heard under the house. They now made sense.

"You know, Lottie wrote to me with pictures and stories about you. I was so proud of the young woman you became. More recently, she told me it was time to come back to Savannah and meet you. And in her last letter, she insisted by sending me an airplane plane ticket."

"And you came to town and went straight to the funeral, didn't you?"

"Yes. And I stood in the back while you gave a eulogy, dying to meet you." Agnes laid her head over on her grandmother's shoulder, letting the story take root in her mind until Gladys announced, "I'm leaving Savannah. It's time for me to go home."

Fear overtook Agnes, but it came out with the sound of anger. "Savannah's your home, and you just got here. We've barely gotten to know one another."

A small grin played across Gladys' face. "I know, sweetheart, but I have a life on Prince Edward Island and a husband to get home to, your grandfather. I was hoping I could talk you into coming back with me. You could visit where I work in Charlottetown and meet your family in Cavendish. You could even bring your mom or a friend if you'd like."

Agnes thought for a minute before answering. "I'm not sure, Gladys. I'm trying to get the restaurant off the ground," she answered, which was true, but it was much more than that. As much as she had loved getting to know Gladys, Agnes was happy. She loved her family and friends and was finally settling into her life back in Savannah. She also felt like something big was happening with Matthew. However, when she saw the disappointment play across Gladys' face, she knew she must put her feelings aside. This lady, her grandmother, had overcome so many obstacles for her. She couldn't let her down. "You know, I haven't opened the doors of the restaurant yet, so it's a perfect time to go." She felt the knot in her stomach the second those words spilled out.

Agnes walked Gladys back home along the bluff. The small, two-lane road was always in need of repair, either from the roots of the majestic oak trees that covered it or the greedy tides that took a little more dirt from its bank each day. Still, it was magical, and it was a great day for meandering. For the first time since Agnes had met Gladys, she seemed at ease. She had told her secrets, and now it was up to those around her to accept them.

"Have you missed Savannah?" Agnes asked.

Gladys was lost in thought, glancing out over the river. Instead of answering Agnes' question, she pointed to a spot in the marsh and remarked, "Barbee's Pavilion was right there. Do you know about it?"

Agnes shook her head, so Gladys explained, "Savannah was once connected by streetcars. As the city's population increased, the streetcar lines' arms stretched further to incorporate more places for its residents' accessibility to the city. The farthest reach was Isle of Hope.

There were two cars a day to get there, morning and night. The one streetcar would travel the long distance, and once it hit Isle of Hope, the driver would walk to the opposite end of the car, flip the 45-degree-angled seats to face in the direction it had just come, then travel back. One of the drivers was Alexander Marcus Barbee.

Mr. Barbee would always stop the streetcar so he wouldn't run over the native turtles on the Island. Eventually, his curiosity got the better of him, and after much research, he realized those turtles were diamond-back terrapins and known as a delicacy worldwide. He settled right here and opened the only terrapin farm in the world. He did quite well for himself, but his keen eye for business kept him moving forward. He enjoyed making Barbee's a place to bring your family. It included a swimming pool, an ice cream stand, a skating rink, a theater, and finally, a dance hall. In fact, Johnny Mercer himself was known to dance the Charleston at Barbee's. Remember when I told you I had met him? It was right here, on this spot."

Gladys had stopped walking completely, her blank eyes looking back to another time.

Agnes nudged her. "Gladys?" But she didn't move. The look on her face scared Agnes, so she grabbed both her shoulders and gave a little shake. "Gladys? Are you okay?" This time, the shake stunned her back to reality.

"I'm sorry," Gladys said, as a tear ran down her cheek. Agnes helped her over to a bench, looking out on the river. She sat quiet, wringing her hands, then turned to Agnes. "You asked if I've missed Savannah. Yes. But, you see, this is not my Savannah. I never saw things run their course. I remember people and places but never grieved their passing or closing. To me, I came back and everything was just gone. That's been the hardest part of this trip. And I realized that even though I was born in Savannah, it's no longer my home. Prince Edward Island is."

Agnes watched as the older woman's eyes grew heavy. "Gladys, I'm gonna run back and get my car to get you home, okay? I'll be right back." Gladys only nodded, then gave in to her tiredness. On the way back to her house, Agnes thought about Gladys' story. She had seen pictures of Barbee's Pavilion before. Still, there was something Gladys wasn't sharing with her. Something that exhausted her to think about. Out of the blue, Agnes pictured her uncle Benjamin. But in her thoughts, he wasn't standing with Aunt Lottie. He was standing with Gladys.

27

GOD WINK

Agnes thought long and hard about visiting Gladys on Prince Edward Island. Truth be known, she was contemplating not going. Something in her gut had been worrying her about her mom. None of her siblings had ever gone in search of their birth parents, so chasing after her grandmother was terrifying.

However, once she learned about Prince Edward Island, she felt like she'd been given a God Wink. That's what she had always called those special moments when God gives you that little bit of verification you need. The fact that Gary, her new friend from the Oyster Stew Crew, had given it to her still surprised her. But once he told her about the oysters on PEI, she remembered the address inside Lottie's box. God Wink.

Researching the oysters would also move her trip from just a visit to a business trip. Lottie's oyster stew was a significant money factor for her company, and the many people who made the stew depended on her. She needed help with the oysters; she knew she lacked experience. But who could help?

Matthew's face flooded her mind. "Oh no. We haven't been dating long enough for me to ask him to travel with me," she muttered aloud. "Are we even dating at all?" she added. But in her heart, she knew the answer. Even if they hadn't made it official, she knew. They were on the fast track to falling in love.

The idea of dating Matthew was fun, but the reality of being in a relationship was terrifying. They had seen each other almost every day since their first boat ride, but they were definitely still in the "getting-to-know-each-other" phase. Would a trip to another country together throw off their balance? Could she find someone else to take to Cavendish? "Yes, I could find someone else," she whispered aloud, but she knew in her heart there was no one else in the world she'd rather take than Matthew.

Agnes' mom kept a firm schedule. It hadn't changed much since when she was a young girl. Every night, after dinner, she would go on a walk. Like a creature of habit, she always tried to leave her house at 7:00 p.m. So, that evening, Agnes was waiting for her mom beside their mailbox. Her mom stepped out the front door at 7:04. She slowly walked down their sidewalk, fiddling with the zipper on her jacket, and almost ran into Agnes.

"Agnes Marie! You scared me half-to-death," she cried out, holding her hand to her chest while leaning in for a peck on the cheek.

"You're running late tonight, Mom. It's 7:04. Mind if I walk with you? I've been trying out recipes and eating all day, I could use the exercise—and the company."

Her mom reached for her hand, "I'm late because your dad couldn't find the remote control and insisted I had it last. I found it beside him in the recliner. And yes, I'd love for you to walk with me, but you'll have to slow your pace for your old mama."

Agnes knew that her mom walked at a quick pace. She sometimes was out of breath trying to keep up, especially when she tried to talk, but she nodded just the same.

They took off on the usual route, walking the sidewalks around the Ardsley Park neighborhood until they came to Hull Park. Her mom circled the park five times before beginning the trip home. As they started loop three, Agnes began. "So, Gladys left yesterday morning. She should be safely back home by now. And....," she stammered, "asked me to visit her on Prince Edward Island."

Her mom quietly answered, "Well, that's nice," which was an odd reply because her mom always had a lot to say.

Agnes glanced over to notice the look on her mom's face; she was deep in thought. Agnes wanted to know those thoughts, so she came right out and asked, "What are you thinking, Mom?"

The question seemed to surprise her mom. She slowed her walking pace before answering. "I don't really know, Agnes. Your father and I have always talked so openly with you and your brothers about your birth families, but to be quite frank with you, we are in uncharted waters. Over and above that, I can't help but be angry that Lottie never told me Gladys was alive. Her son would have been my cousin. I somehow feel a loss for something I never had in the beginning. Gladys has always just been a tombstone at Bonaventure." Her mom stopped walking and turned to face Agnes. "Gladys just swept into Savannah out of the blue and now threatens to upend my baby's world. It scares the hell out of me, and I don't want you to get hurt." A tear began falling down her face, but she never dropped her gaze from Agnes. "I know moms are supposed to be strong, and I truly want what's best for you. That's all I've ever wanted for all of my children. Even if what's best might mean not living in Savannah with me."

Agnes began to cry right along with her mom. "You don't

have to worry about that. I'm not moving. I just want to know more. So, when Gladys asked me to visit her on Prince Edward Island, I said yes. But I wanted to run all this by you before I made any plans. You know how much I love you, don't you?"

"I never doubted it. The funny thing about love is there is always room for more. It's not like a cup of water where there is only a certain amount; it is an endless pool." She pushed back a strand of Agnes' hair, sticking to the tears on her face, then softly added, "You know, just because Gladys asked you to visit doesn't mean you have to go. Is this something you want to do?"

Agnes nodded. "She's old, Mom. If I have any questions, I need to find the answers now. I don't mean to be morbid, but who knows how long I have with her. But I don't want to go without your support."

"Oh, Agnes. You have my support, one hundred percent," her mom said with a smile as they continued walking the lap.

"You know, I've never asked you before. What made you start adopting?"

"Your dad and I always wanted a large family. But when we began to try and get pregnant, it never happened. We went to a fertility specialist who only scratched the surface and said he didn't see any glaring reasons why we weren't. We were doing NFP, so I knew my fertile times. But after a year, we still weren't pregnant. We decided that if we were open to life, it wouldn't matter where that life came from. So, we went through the process to become adoptive parents, put our fertility in God's hands, and continued to pray for a family. Then, one day, the door opened."

"After adopting Tim, we assumed we wouldn't be chosen again, but we kept our file updated and continued to pray for the family God wanted us to have. I truly believe that God gives us the children He wishes us to have, and we were blessed with each of you." She reached over and squeezed Agnes' hand. "And you continue to bless us every day."

Agnes's heart was full of love and gratitude for having such amazing parents. "I hope I can be as wonderful a parent as you."

Her mom smiled at the comment, but her attention returned to the subject at hand. "Okay, back to your trip to Canada. I wish you weren't going alone."

Agnes looked sheepishly at her mom. "I'm thinking of asking Matthew to go with me."

Her mom's eyebrows shot up as she once again stopped walking. "Matthew Monroe?"

Agnes nodded as a small smile moved across her lips.

"I thought you shut that door completely after Guatemala. I need to hear more about how Matthew got you to reopen that door," her mom teased. She kissed her daughter on her forehead before adding, "You know I always liked that boy." Then she linked her arm through Agnes' as they slowly walked home.

28

COMPARING STEWS

Agnes' thoughts drifted to Matthew, and she felt the familiar tingle in her stomach. She and Matthew had been seeing each other for weeks, and each greeting always began with a kiss. Agnes wondered if she would always be weak in the knees from the feel of his lips on hers. One thing was for certain, each kiss was becoming more and more intense. Each one pulled the air from her lungs and left her stunned for several minutes afterward.

Something drew her attention back to the clock. She gasped when she realized she had been daydreaming for a long time; she was now five minutes past the time she wanted to begin. She hurried around the kitchen until everything was perfect.

Matthew walked in without knocking. "Is anybody home?" he called out, but immediately added, "It smells amazing in here."

The sound of his voice made her heart quicken. *He walked into my house without knocking.* He'd been over to her house several times, but this was the first time he'd walked straight in. It felt so personal; she relished in the warmth of the familiarity.

"I'm in the kitchen; come on back," she answered, but nothing ever prepared her for the feeling she got in her stomach when they finally saw each other. It was almost magical.

"I brought you something," he said, holding up a bouquet of pink camellias tied with a piece of twine.

"Did you steal those from your mama's big camellia bush by the road?" she asked.

"Uh, maybe I did, maybe I didn't," he answered with a laugh. "But you can't prove a thing."

"They're beautiful. Thank you," she said with a smile.

"Don't I get something in return?" he asked, puckering up and leaning in.

Moving in ever so slightly, she whispered in her sexiest voice, "Yes, dinner."

He watched her lips as she spoke, then returned his gaze to her eyes. Her breath caught as she felt the steam between them. She couldn't fight the pull any longer. Their lips met in the perfect kiss. His arm reached around to her back, pulling her closer. His smell and his taste caused her to physically ache for him in a way she had never experienced before. And just like that, she was lost.

The smell of smoke broke the spell. She jumped back from him, almost as if she'd been burnt instead of the flounder. She turned her attention to the other fire in the room, the fish on the stovetop. Quickly removing the iron skillet from the flame, she scooped up her crispy-scored flounder just in time to save it from imminent danger.

Matthew followed closely and hugged her from behind, peeking around to investigate the meal. She had pulled her dark hair into a high bun, exposing her neck. Matthew found her weak spot and immediately began kissing it. She closed her eyes, letting the sensation run through her body until the oil in the skillet began to sizzle loudly once again.

She shook her head, trying to pull her brain back into the present. With a hoarse voice, she mumbled, "I think we need a chaperone."

Taking a deep breath, he pulled himself free from her and backed away slowly until he hit the counter on the other side of the kitchen. "You might be right," he said. Then, with a wicked grin, he added, "But what fun would that be?"

She smiled but motioned him to the table. "Why don't you open the wine and have a seat. The first course will be out soon."

They talked briefly about their day until Agnes brought out the oyster stew. It was one of the last batches made with PEI Oysters. Matthew's face lit up when she placed it in front of him. "This looks like Lottie's Famous Oyster Stew. I grew up eating this but haven't had it for years. Where did you buy it from?"

Agnes beamed with pride, "I own it. Lottie's been making and shipping it all over the U.S. for years."

"No way, Agnes. That's incredible," Matthew said with pride.

"Yes, it is. But I have one problem, and I hope you can help me. You see, Lottie wanted to start making the stew with local oysters but couldn't locate anyone who could supply her with the needed amount. So, she found the nearest source, which was in Florida." She pulled the soup bowl away from Matthew and replaced it with another full bowl of stew. "Try this," she instructed.

Matthew stirred the piping hot stew, then scooped up a spoonful with an oyster. "Hmm," he grunted, swirling the liquid and then taking another bite. "It's not bad, but it doesn't taste like Lottie's. Most oysters in the Atlantic waterways are the same type, but the taste changes depending on where it's grown. The ones near us tend to have a lemongrass flavor, whereas oysters in Florida taste differently. But these are smaller. They probably were disturbed from the big hurricane a couple of months ago, and they had to pull them early."

"That's what my Oyster Stew Crew said. So, you agree that we're right to say that the stew is now much different?"

Matthew nodded. "Oyster Stew Crew?" he asked with a smirk.

Agnes' face reddened. She had named them but had never said it out loud. "They are the most amazing group of cooks, and they're local; you're gonna love them," she remarked, then returned to business. "Lottie's notes from her original recipe said she bought local oysters from a man in Isle of Hope, who I assume was Mr. Louey, that you worked for. But her notes changed later, saying she had to find another source when he got older and quit. I wasn't sure why she bought them from Canada until recently."

She had Matthew's full attention, so she gave him a brief explanation of her adoption and her grandmother living on Prince Edward Island. "I think that the oysters being purchased from there is no coincidence, but I don't know enough about oysters to verify any of this."

Matthew slid the first bowl back in front of him and took another bite. "This really is great oyster stew. How can I help?"

Butterflies took over her insides as she drew up the courage to ask. What's the worst thing he can do, say no? "My grandmother wants me to come and visit her on Prince Edward Island. Would you come with me?"

The question floated in the air for what seemed like an eternity. She was about to withdraw the offer when he answered, "I'd love to." Then he added, "We need to go soon if you want to get a good look at the oysters; it freezes pretty early."

"Freezes?" she asked.

"Oh, yeah. The oyster farmers submerge their baskets close to the ocean floor before it ices over."

Agnes shivered, remembering the cold in Indiana and not wanting to get back into it. Nevertheless, she had things that must be done, and this time, she had Matthew with her to tackle the obstacles and, most importantly, to keep her warm.

29

ALL SAINTS DAY

Agnes arrived at church early to save space for her friends. All Saints' Day noon Mass was always packed with downtown workers and Catholics who couldn't make the early Mass before work.

As the tribe arrived one by one, they began to search for Agnes, who had agreed to save them seats. They found her in the middle of the far-left section. The pews on the sides were smaller than those running down the middle and only held three people. So, Agnes had spread the contents of her purse across both pews. She angrily fought off the Holy Mass-goers who tried to push her wallet, brush, and emergency sanitary products to the side in order to sit before the mass bells rang.

By the time her friends found her, she was so worked up that she snapped at them: "Oh, great. Y'all come strolling in here thirty seconds before Mass, expecting me to save you a seat. I should make you stand in the back with all the other slackers." Agnes pointed to the line of people beginning to find their place along the back wall.

Kathleen picked up the items from the seat and then turned to Agnes, holding up the maxi-pad. "Really, Agnes?"

"Hey, don't complain. This Mass runs over an hour, and you've got a seat, don't you?"

Kathleen raised her eyebrows but continued to hold up the sanitary product. She then added loudly enough for the whole group to hear, "You can have this back. I won't be needing any of these for the next eight months."

They all turned to her in shock as the cathedral's organ silenced them with the opening hymn, each quietly holding in their emotions as much as possible during church. But when the sign of peace came, they began hugging. They talked so excitedly that they hadn't realized Mass had continued. All eyes turned to them, staring them into silence. Still, they continued to hold each other's hands. One of them was pregnant. It was certainly something that should be celebrated—just not during church.

As soon as the priest walked out the massive church doors, the group clung to one another. Making their way to the exit, they huddled outside. Finally, Kathleen said, "I'm getting hangry. You've got to feed this pregnant person soon." So, they decided to walk to the nearby Mrs. Wilkes. They were seated at a table for ten, which was the standard table size in the homey restaurant that felt like someone's dining room. Wallpapered walls and family pictures decorated the room. The only thing bringing it to the modern world was the automatic cash machine in the corner. A family of four visiting Savannah from Texas was seated with the tribe. The mom, not much older than the group, seemed very uncomfortable sharing her space but still offered a smile.

Mrs. Wilkes was known for its delicious Southern-style food, which gave the feeling of sitting around the table as a family. The dishes were brought out one by one, and the guests passed them around, taking what they wanted.

The group idly chit-chatted while passing the tray of fried chicken, bowls of macaroni-and-cheese, field peas, white rice, squash casserole, butter beans, sweet potato soufflé, okra gumbo and biscuits, just to name a few. Everyone searched for an empty space on the table to leave the dish once it had been passed to everyone. Agnes always enjoyed the feel of the room with the sound of friendly conversation flowing over the passing of dishes. She had never pinpointed the reason before, but now that she would run her own restaurant, she wondered if it would have the same homey feeling.

While the tribe talked about their upcoming weekend, their parental table mates cut up and served the children their food, then quickly turned to their plates to take bites. The minute the children were done, they became rowdy. The parents tried to quiet them, but the children wanted no part in it. Finally, the husband stood, telling his wife he would take the children outside to run around while she finished her meal. She watched as they walked out the door, then quickly turned to her food and shoveled it into her mouth. When she looked up, she noticed all the ladies' eyes were on her, and her face went crimson.

"I don't remember the last time I enjoyed a meal," she said. "Wait, it was five years ago, the day before my first child was born," she added. "Enjoy it now, ladies. Because once you have kids, you don't get a moment to yourself." She wiped her mouth quickly, set her napkin on the table, and said goodbye, leaving the tribe looking from one to the other.

"Surely, she's over-exaggerating," Kathleen said. "My mom never acted like that."

"Not to you, she didn't, because you were one of those children," Jan replied. Maggie kicked her hard under the table, and Jan yelped in response. "What? You know that's the truth," she snipped at Maggie.

Kathleen inhaled loudly while instinctively touching her stomach. The tribe began to try to ease her worries, offering her advice they had zero knowledge about until Kathleen announced, "Thank you for all worrying about me, but I'm fine." A small smile moved across her face. "Actually, I'm better than fine. Jack and I are having a baby. And no over-stressed mother on vacation will make me worry about something I can no longer control. Now, help me wave down our waiter. Today, I'm ready for some peach cobbler."

The table moved back to casual conversation. Agnes took the opportunity to tell them her news: "I've got something to share with you guys. Remember I'd mentioned the friend of Lottie's who had come to her funeral?" They all nodded. Well, it turns out she's actually my birth grandmother." She was met by looks of confusion.

"What in the hell does that even mean?" Latrice asked.

Agnes laughed nervously. "It means her son was my birthfather."

"Was?" Stephanie asked.

Agnes nodded. "My parents asked me over last week, and Gladys was there. She shared with me how my birth mother and father both died when I was an infant. She told me she wasn't able to raise me, so she brought me to the only family she had, which was here, in Savannah." Her friends continued to stare at her in confusion until Kathleen spoke.

"I'm so sorry, Agnes. I know you don't talk about your adoption often, but I'm so sorry your birth parents have passed away."

Everyone at the table chimed in while Maggie reached over and held her hand.

"Thank you so much, but I'm fine, really. It's been nice getting to know Gladys and learning the truth. In fact, she wants me to come to Prince Edward Island and meet her husband's family, and I've decided to go."

"You shouldn't go alone. Do you want one of us to go with you?" Kathleen asked.

"Oh, I'm not going alone," she spit out before she realized

what she had done. She sat for a brief second, hoping no one had caught her slip. But looking into their eyes, she knew she would need to explain further. "Matthew Monroe is going with me."

The table burst with sound: questions, comments, and one little "Whoo-Whoo."

"All right, all right. It's not like that," Agnes scolded.

Latrice, who was always the interrogator, asked, "Are y'all romantically involved?"

"I'm pleading the fifth," Agnes answered.

"I take that as a yes," Latrice stated.

"No," Agnes interjected.

"No, you don't have feelings for him?" Latrice asked.

"I'm calling 'bullshit' on that," Stephanie interjected. "You've had feelings for Matthew for as long as we can remember."

Agnes rolled her eyes. "You guys are impossible. Yes, Matthew and I have been seeing each other a bit. And I really like him. But I asked him to go to Prince Edward Island to help me with a problem I'm having at work with oysters. So, now you know. I'll be gone a few weeks, and I'll miss you guys."

Jan piped up, "I have a dumb question." Agnes turned her attention directly to her, asking, "Where is Prince Edward Island?"

Agnes laughed. "I'm so sorry. It's in Canada."

Jan thought for a second, then replied. "Do you know what's crazy? If none of that tragedy had happened with your birth parents, you would be Canadian. We would never have known you." The table went quiet as they leaned in closer until Jan added, "Eh?"

Everyone laughed and joined in. "You wouldn't have gone to Notre Dame, eh?"

"And you wouldn't have met Matthew, eh?"

"And our lives wouldn't be the same, eh?"

"I love you guys," Agnes announced as she looked around the table at her tribe. Each one smiled and wiped their eyes.

They were brought back to reality when the waiter approached their table cautiously. "I've got just the thing that will help a table full of crying females," he said with a smile, holding out his tray. "Cobbler and pudding. And today, I'll let you grab one of each."

30

WHEN THE LIGHTS GO OUT

Agnes had clothes spread across her bed; she had no idea what to pack. Luckily, she had lived in the cold before, so she threw in a couple of pairs of jeans and pulled down her heavy coat and boots from the top of her closet. Then she remembered the famous layering trick, so she packed some thinner tops and a couple of light sweaters.

She stopped when she heard the horses. They sounded like they were under her window, and the noises almost seemed like a warning. She jumped when she heard the knock on the door. The sound of the horses stopped at that exact moment, making it even more startling.

Her stomach tightened, and she slowly peeked around her bedroom door to look down the long hallway. The three sets of eyes made contact with hers and began to yell at her.

"Come on, Agnes. Let us in," her brother yelled out.

Relief washed over her as she walked down the hallway, but they continued yelling impatiently.

"Oh, come on!" her other brother called.

"We're growing old here," the third one added.

She smiled and began walking slower, pretending her legs

were made of lead just to irritate them. They banged one last time before she got to the door. As soon as the lock clicked open, they burst through the door, grabbing, tickling, and teasing.

"This place hasn't changed a bit," Bobby said as he turned into the living room and sat heavily on the couch.

"At least it doesn't smell the same. Remember how it always smelled like Lottie," Tim added.

Agnes took a deep breath. "Thank you for saying that; I was worried that I couldn't smell it anymore. What are y'all up to?"

"Mom made spaghetti, so we all went over for dinner, and she was telling us you were leaving for Canada tomorrow. The whole thing is crazy. Can you believe Lottie kept that from everybody?"

"No. I wish she would have told me before Gladys did, but I know she had her reasons," Agnes answered.

Her brother, Chris, interjected, "We're proud of you, sis. This was a lot to take in. We talked about it on the way over and agreed that we'd be freaked out if it happened to us. We just want you to know. Well . . ." He stumbled with his words.

Tim finished, "We want you to know we love you."

Agnes' heart was so full. Her brothers had always looked out for her. She kissed each of them on the cheek, thanking them for riding over. But they were interrupted by someone else coming in the door.

"Hey, I'm looking for the sexy woman that lives here," Matthew called out.

Agnes cringed, but all three of her brothers shot to their feet. When Matthew turned the corner into the living room, her brothers stood tall with their chests puffed out. The look on Matthew's face said it all, but he quickly tried to explain.

"Hey, wait a minute. I was just teasing Agnes. Guns down, men," he called out.

"Matthew? What are you doing here? And why are you walking right into Agnes' house?" Bobby asked.

Matthew turned to Agnes, who stood to explain, "So, Matthew and I are..." she floundered, not knowing quite what to say.

Matthew finished, "We're dating. Agnes and I are dating."

Agnes felt the tingle in her stomach as she walked over to Matthew and kissed him on the cheek. She was shocked at how naturally Matthew had told them as if it were common knowledge. He wasn't intimidated or embarrassed; he claimed his feelings. She was beaming.

Bobby walked over and shook his hand, and the others followed. "That's great news." Then, looking down at them holding hands, he added, "You two look great together."

Everyone sat back down and began talking, except for Tim. He was a wanderer. He began to circle the room, inspecting the trinkets Agnes had placed on the table. He stopped at a desk near the window and began looking at an old map that was sitting open. "What's this, Agnes?"

"I found that in Lottie's office in the shed. It's an old map of the property," she answered.

"Lottie has an office in the shed?" Chris asked.

Agnes looked at each of them, all waiting for her answer, and decided to let them in on her secret. Well, part of her secret. They didn't need to know she could speak to dead horses. That part could wait. "Yes, you're not gonna believe what the shed looks like. Want to see?" They all agreed. "Let me grab my jacket. I'll meet you out back," she said.

Two minutes later, when she walked out the back door, she was surrounded by fog, and there was no sign of her brothers or Matthew. She began to call out for them as she slowly walked toward the back of the lot. Finally, on the third try, someone answered. Following their voices, she walked toward the shed and found them clumped together near the side.

"What's up with this fog?" Bobby asked.

"They call this area the Mystic," Agnes explained.

"The Mystic? What the hell does that mean?"

"That means they have no idea why it fogs up so often," Agnes explained. "Or, what lies beneath it."

Tim didn't wander off this time. His eyes widened as he stared into the thick fog enclosing them together. "I think I'm good not going to see Lottie's office," he said.

Agnes laced her arm through his. "It's okay. I promise," she whispered and pulled him along.

Agnes had been there several times and knew her way well. They walked to the opposite side of the shed. Opening the door, she walked inside and turned on the lights as the others followed.

"Wow. I never would have thought that nasty, vine-covered shed would be so chic inside," Bobby announced. They each agreed, voicing their surprise.

Agnes slowly showed them around the room, filling them in on the many things she had found. She stopped when she got to the closet door that led to the slave hiding place, wondering if she should show them. She remembered when she and her brothers would explore different areas and knew they would love to see it, so she began. "Okay, I want to show you something, but you have to promise not to freak out." She should have known that telling a group of boys not to freak out only excited them, and they eagerly begged her to share her information. Opening the door, she flipped on the light switch. Each of them looked down the uneven stairs and slowly backed away, one at a time, except for Chris.

"Have you been down there?" he asked.

"I sure have," Agnes answered.

"What's down there?" he asked while the others begged her for more information.

"You're gonna have to find out yourself," she teased, making her way to the back of the group.

The most curious brother went first, then the others followed, turning the lights on as they descended. When they finally reached the bottom, they walked into the dirt-floored room, and she followed. They began to pelt her with questions. The final one was, "Do you think Lottie's husband's family hid runaway slaves?" And the answer they all decided upon was, "Yes!"

And then the room went dark. Pitch. Black. Dark.

Everyone began yelling at once. "Hey, turn the light on." "What just happened?" "Help!"

Agnes heard the small voices at the top of the stairs and shushed the group.

"Is anybody down there?" her mom called out.

"Mom, you turned the light off. Can you turn it back on?" The room filled with light, and everyone whooped in happiness. A few seconds later, her mom and dad turned the corner. "What are you doing here?" Agnes asked.

"I told the boys I was bringing over dessert for everyone to enjoy before you left town," she answered, turning to Matthew and adding, "Hello, Matthew." She then began asking the same questions the rest of the group had and came up with the same answers. Finally, her mom shivered. "This place is freezing. Let's go back to the main house for coffee and dessert."

Everybody fled except for Agnes and Matthew.

"I guess the cat is out the bag about us now, huh?" Matthew asked.

"Yeah, and my brothers know you think I'm sexy," Agnes added.

He slowly leaned over and kissed her in between his fragmented sentences. "You" Kiss. "Are." Kiss. "So sexy," he finished.

Once again, her mom turned the lights off at the top of the stairs. Agnes and Matthew welcomed the darkness and their time alone until she heard the sound in the back of the room and went rigid.

"What is it? Does the darkness scare you?"

She didn't answer. She only listened and could swear she heard people whispering in the back of the room. When the lights came back on, she began to explain but was cut off.

"Sorry—again," her mom called out, but Agnes didn't respond. She was searching the back of the room and wasn't surprised to find it completely empty.

31

WELCOME TO PRINCE EDWARD ISLAND

Agnes watched out the window as the plane descended. She was surprised to see an orange tint under the water. "That looks like Georgia red clay," she murmured, looking over at Matthew, who was still sleeping. Glancing back out the window, she noticed a white lighthouse sitting on a patch of green looking over a rocky coastline, but the dirt road leading to the lighthouse was bright orange. She remembered being taught that the red color came from the high iron content soil and wondered if all of Prince Edward Island was similar.

The Charlottetown airport was surprisingly busy for its size. They disembarked onto the tarmac and were ushered into the building. Agnes had never been to Canada before and thought the island would feel foreign, but at every turn, she felt like she was in any airport in the United States. After picking up their rented car, they followed the directions into Charlottetown. They were surprised that the quaint city had such a small-town feel while having many business areas. Pulling out the address Gladys had sent them, they followed one of the many long, straight roads, counting the building numbers until they were in the one-hundred block that ran right into the river.

The four-story, red brick building had been modernized with a new entryway and windows, but the beauty of the historic structure underneath was still apparent. It reminded Agnes of Savannah, where they held on to their history while making updates for the present.

The black iron sign above the door read "The O'Hara Center of Nursing" in gold lettering. Passing under, Agnes wondered if the O'Hara who began it was any relation to Gladys. Once inside, they passed a group of nursing students referring to a schedule hanging in the reception area, then proceeded to the receptionist.

"Hi. Could you please direct me to the office of Gladys O'Hara?"

The receptionist seemed surprised. "Do you have an appointment?"

Agnes looked to Matthew, who shrugged. "No, but she's expecting me."

"May I get your name, please?" the receptionist asked firmly but not angrily.

"My name is Agnes Reed."

The lady flipped through pages in an appointment book, then replied, "I don't see your name anywhere. Would you be listed under another name?"

Agnes hesitated, then answered with a question. "Her granddaughter?"

This got the receptionist's attention, and she jumped to her feet. "Oh. Hello. Let me show you to her office." Turning to the second receptionist, she announced she would be back shortly. Then, she walked around the desk quickly and motioned for Agnes and Matthew to follow.

Walking down the main hall, they turned into a private hallway and into a cozy waiting room. "Please wait here. I'll only be a minute," they were told before the receptionist disappeared down the hallway.

"It's so nice in here," Matthew stated, walking from one picture to the next, observing its subjects. Agnes came to stand beside him and laced her hand into his. Suddenly, she was nervous about seeing Gladys again but wasn't sure why. When she looked at the photo that Matthew was inspecting, she saw Gladys. It was a much younger version of herself, but definitely her. The plaque beneath read, "Opening day of O'Hara School of Nursing with honorary guest Gladys O'Hara."

"Oh my gosh, that's my grandma," Agnes pointed out to Matthew.

"That has a sweet ring to it," someone said from behind. Agnes spun around to find Gladys standing in the doorway. She walked to her quickly and gave her a hug. "I've been waiting for that hug all day," she added, "and it was worth the wait."

Agnes pulled back and introduced Matthew.

"Oh yes, the oysterer," Gladys announced.

Matthew looked at Agnes questioningly, and she shrugged.

"Lottie told me about you," Gladys explained. She and Agnes exchanged looks, and a small grin moved across Agnes' face.

"I have no idea what you're referring to," Matthew answered. "But it's nice to meet you, Mrs. O'Hara."

"You as well, Matthew. Please, come on back to my office."

They walked down the hallway and into a lush, nautical-themed office with overstuffed leather chairs. Behind the desk was a wall of windows that looked across the rooftops of many houses, all the way down to the river. But the most impressive thing in the room was the nameplate on Gladys' desk that read "Gladys O'Hara—Founder."

"You're famous," Agnes said.

"Not really. I was just good at what I did, and that was nursing. When I moved here from Savannah, I took up where I left off with my nursing classes. After Henri was born, I worked my way up in the ranks and held down our local hospital while many of our local nurses went to serve in the war. Some didn't make it back home." She paused. Her eyes lost their focus for a split second, then re-connected. "The ones that did usually didn't return to the hospital. They had seen enough blood to last them a lifetime. At any rate, I was recognized for my ability to handle crises, especially trauma. They asked me to teach others, and I did. I taught many, many others. That led to this." She motioned to the office around her.

"This is amazing, Gladys," Agnes said.

"It's not half as amazing as my granddaughter standing before me," she said with a smile.

"Now, let me show you around the building a little bit, and then we'll walk to get some lunch." Gladys took them floor by floor, explaining bits and pieces of her life as they explored. The building itself was beautiful, but the way it had been modernized for the nursing classes was ingenious.

"We graduate hundreds of registered nurses and registered psychiatric nurses each year. We are part of Charlottetown College but are in collaboration with three other nursing programs that send their nursing students to us for the final two years of education," she explained as they passed many students and teachers in the hallways who all said hello. Gladys called them each by name and even asked some of them personal questions about their day. When she noticed Agnes watching her, she said, "We all get very close here."

They ended their tour on the fourth floor on an old "lookout porch" with views of the river. The cold November wind took Agnes' breath away, reminding her of the cold in Indiana. But the view captured her. She could see the expanse of the town below, the large harbor on the other side, and then to the hillsides. "Charlottetown is beautiful. This looks like a postcard," Agnes remarked.

"Yes, it is beautiful," Gladys answered. "But this isn't the best thing about Charlottetown; it's our food. Are you hungry?"

"Starving," Agnes answered.

"Then let me grab my bag and let's go." Gladys stopped by her office, and they began their walk toward the harbor.

Like many other towns along the Eastern Seaboard, Charlottetown was set up in the typical grid pattern. It reminded Agnes of Savannah, with its beautiful historic district and the main focal point of the harbor. She and Matthew walked slowly, observing the sites on each block, while Gladys clipped along ahead of them, taking the path she'd walked so many times before. When they reached the waterway, they made their way onto what Gladys described as food trucks on floating docks. They stepped slowly down the gangway to a large area on the floating floor. There were many restaurants and bars to choose from. Everything from fried seafood, burgers, tacos, and lobster rolls were available at the many stands.

Each ordered different seafood dishes and carried them to one of the several center tables. Gladys then walked over to the bar and came back with three of their local craft beers. Agnes was worried about being cold, but the floating dock was sitting down in the water of a low tide, so it kept them warm and protected by its surrounding bluff. Agnes took a bite of a shrimp taco, washed it down with a sip of beer, then turned her face up at the sun. "Hmmmm," she murmured as a satisfied smile crossed her face. "This is such a good day."

Matthew agreed and silently placed his hand on top of Agnes'.

Gladys watched the scene and then turned her face up to the sun, too. "You're so right; this is a very good day."

32

ONE-HALF

Matthew drove slowly while Agnes scanned the numbers on the houses, looking for 52 ½. After lunch, Gladys had given them directions before she went back to work. They were to settle into what she referred to as a small apartment behind the main house, but as they pulled in front of the three-story building, it was anything but. The house sat right off the street. The only thing between it and the road was the sidewalk that ran around the island. A bright yellow door stood out against its steel blue tiles, inviting visitors to come in for a visit.

How could this be the "little place in the city" that Gladys referred to? Agnes wondered. She turned the knob to the front door and found it open, so she pocketed the key Gladys had given them and stepped inside the entryway. The smell of Murphy's Oil Soap hit her immediately, making her glance down at the heart pine floors, which were worn with time. The inside was more modern than she expected, but the original qualities had been preserved and modernized. Arched doorways split on each side, one side entering a living room with a stacked slate fireplace. The other doorway entered directly into a kitchen with white cabinets and subway tiles with a pop of green on the island that matched the metal shade of the pendant lights.

"Wow," Agnes muttered, comparing the massive kitchen to her small galley kitchen in Savannah. "Gladys really knows how to do it up right, huh?"

"It's beautiful, but somehow, the house doesn't seem to match its owner unless we really don't know its owner well," Matthew remarked.

Agnes shot him a look as they continued walking through the kitchen, but as always, Agnes was distracted by the smell of food. She followed her nose to find chicken covered in a cream sauce cooking in a crockpot. She thought it odd that Gladys had put such a large amount of food in the slow cooker but shook it off and continued to the refrigerator. "Oh yeah," she whispered when she saw a Coke on the top shelf, and guiltily pulled it out and popped it open.

The house was three stories tall, with four bedrooms on the second floor and the master suite on the top floor. They struggled to open the French doors, whose frame seemed to be warped. But the view was worth all the effort once they thrust them open. They had a bird's-eye view of the city itself, with the main focus on the cathedral. Many spotlights beamed up its sides, highlighting the arches and bell tower. But in the open spaces, the town itself was settling in for the afternoon. As the sun began to set, various lights flickered on to combat the darkness, making Agnes wonder how it might have appeared in a time before electricity with only candles glowing around the city. Her thoughts were interrupted by Matthew pointing to the backyard.

"Hey, what's that?"

Agnes had only been looking out over the city and had not bothered looking straight down. The backyard was covered with a deck and a small house sitting in the back corner with its light on. "Let's go check it out," Agnes suggested, and they quickly retraced their path down the stairs. This time, Agnes noticed several family pictures hanging from the walls with faces of people she had never met. *I don't know any of these people*, she thought sadly but continued moving along.

Once on ground level, they crossed to the back of the house and walked onto the back deck. They wandered around, looking at various outdoor metal signs that had been hung around a bar area. A small door off the back of the house was propped open, showing a closet with garden supplies inside. Agnes noticed a bright pine-straw hat with poppies attached, and she playfully put it on her head as they continued to walk. When they finally returned to the small cottage in the back, they noticed the number 59 ½. Agnes felt a knot tighten in her stomach as they heard the house's back door open. Turning, they found a couple holding a baby with a toddler hiding behind his mother's skirt.

"Oh shit," was all Agnes could say as she slowly pulled the hat from her head and tried to hide the Coke behind her back.

The couple burst out laughing as the family's mom said, "Gladys asked us to watch out for you to make sure you got settled. I see you've found everything."

"I'm so sorry. We got a bit confused," Agnes called back.

"No worries," the mom replied, handing the baby to the dad and walking out into the garden. "It happens all the time, really. It doesn't help that we leave the door unlocked. But that's what we do on the island, so it's a habit. I've known Gladys my whole life. She's so happy you're here. She's talked of nothing else." She pointed to the cottage and added, "If you need anything, let me know. My name is Liz."

Agnes thanked her and pulled the key out of her pocket. She smiled when she walked into a cottage about the same size as hers in Savannah. The entryway was the main living room, with the kitchen sitting in its corner. From where she stood, she could see a small bathroom and two bedrooms on each side. She and Matthew exchanged a look.

"Does this feel more like Gladys?" Matthew asked.

Agnes nodded, "This feels exactly like Gladys. It feels like home." And it became just that for them while they were in Charlottetown. When Gladys came home that afternoon, she found them in the kitchen, playfully cooking dinner for her. Agnes knew her crab cake recipe by heart but had substituted lobster, which was plentiful at the local grocer. She served it on a bed of lettuce with a light lemon vinegar sauce.

Once seated, Gladys teased, "You better watch out. I might never let you leave."

Agnes reached over and squeezed her hand, appreciating the moment between them.

After dinner, Gladys suggested they take a short stroll to walk off dinner. She gave them a full history tour as they walked along Queen Street. Although she had been born in Savannah, Prince Edward Island was obviously her home, and she was proud of it.

Gladys explained, "Founded by the French in the fifteen hundreds, the island was like so many others and was taken over by the British in the mid-eighteenth century. They deported all of the French settlers and later gave the island the name Prince Edward after, well, Prince Edward, Duke of Kent, who was the fourth son of King George III. Many English, Scottish, and Irish settlers left their homeland in large numbers in search of a better life and came to settle in PEI. My husband's family were from Ireland and settled on a section of the island called Cavendish."

Agnes and Matthew exchanged glances, acknowledging the connection to the oysters. Finally, Agnes asked, "Can we go there?"

"Absolutely. I need to be in the city tomorrow, but we will

leave the following morning. In the meantime, you can explore Charlottetown and stay in the cottage."

They continued to walk block by block, getting further away from the tourists. They came upon a three-story, red brick building with a long overhanging roof down its side, providing a covering for anyone waiting. *But what would they be waiting for?* Agnes wondered.

As if on cue, Gladys explained. "This is the old train station, but it's now an office building." They walked under the cover of the overhang held by black iron supports. Underneath was a sign that read, "ATTENTION. Falling snow and ice," with a picture of a stick figure underneath a pile of snow that had fallen off the roof.

"Winter is harsh here. You wouldn't believe how many people get hurt from sliding ice and snow every year," Gladys remarked. "This was my first stop on Prince Edward Island. I never would have made off that train if it wasn't for the sweet, young novice. She was new in the order and had gone to Boston to meet with her superiors. She had people carry me up the road to the hospital. She saved my life. And all she asked me to do in return was marry her fiancé."

33

CAVENDISH

Agnes noticed snow flurries as she and Matthew placed their bags in the back of Gladys' car. The temperature had continued dropping since they arrived on Prince Edward Island, so they weren't surprised. But the map had shown Cavendish as an hour's drive away, so she asked, "What do we do if it starts snowing hard?"

"We keep driving," Gladys answered with a smile. "This isn't Savannah when we reminisce about the year it snowed at Christmas. It snows every year here, and it lasts for months. So don't worry, you're safe."

All of Agnes' worries lifted when Gladys told her she was safe. She knew Gladys could handle the situation. As the car drove out of Charlottetown, Agnes began to replay some of the conversations she had with Gladys over the past couple of days and focused on one in particular.

"Hey Gladys, the other day when you showed us the old train station, you said the young novice who had saved you asked you to marry her fiancé. Did you?" Agnes asked.

Gladys laughed. "I told the young nun 'no,' but she was tricky. She took no for my answer but only if I agreed to go home with her for a weekend. I felt I owed her at least that, so I went home with her once my foot healed. You see, the old man who owned Wexford Oyster Company, your great-grandfather, knew it took lots of strong men to run an oyster farm. His sons seemed uninterested in marrying and only wanted to be out on the water. So, he told them he would only leave the company to one of them if they married before he died."

"You're kidding me. Could he do that?" Agnes asked.

"He couldn't make anyone marry unwillingly, but he could dangle a carrot in front of his boys to get them searching for a wife. Anyway, I didn't know any of this. She only wanted me to meet Patrick. And let's just say we hit it off. And the rest is history."

"You fell in love?" Agnes announced.

"We got along very well together," Gladys corrected. "And still do. We've made each other happy, and above everything else, we kept Wexford Oyster Company going strong for all these years."

"That's nice," Agnes said as she glanced back at Matthew, who was shaking his head in bewilderment.

Gladys changed the conversation as she pointed to a passing sign. "Look. There's the sign for the Green Gables Heritage Place. Would you like to see it on this visit?"

Agnes watched as the sign passed, then asked, "Anne of Green Gables?"

"That's the one," Gladys answered.

Agnes had grown up reading *Anne of Green Gables* and had since watched every movie. She had never once linked Prince Edward Island with Avonlea from the story and suddenly got excited.

"Lucy Maud Montgomery, who wrote the Anne books, was a local author who was inspired by this island. The Green Gables Heritage Place is where you can see it all. Canadians love the fictional character of Anne," Gladys explained.

"Who is Anne of Green Gables?" Matthew asked.

They both turned to him in dismay.

"It's a novel. Have you never heard of it?" Gladys asked.

"Nope," Matthew answered. "Is it one of those chick-lit books?"

"No, it's a classic about a young orphan named Anne who is adopted by an elderly brother and sister and brought to Avonlea to help farm. But people are cruel to her because she's precocious and has a wild imagination and, well, because she has red hair."

Matthew gave her a dead stare. "Does that sound like something I'd enjoy?" When they both laughed, he added. "You need to get me around some men folk soon; how long until we get to Cavendish?"

"It's just a bit further," Gladys answered. She turned to Agnes and said, "I'll take you alone one day. The Heritage Place even has 'Lover's Lane'".

"Awwww," Agnes said, causing Gladys to do the same.

Shaking his head, Matthew added, "Can you drive any faster?"

Ten minutes later, Gladys pulled off the road onto a white driveway made of gravel and crushed oyster shells. They appeared to be driving into the woods until they came upon a clearing. In the distance, they could see water, but the driveway was lined with boxes of some kind.

"Are those oyster baskets?" Matthew asked.

"They are. They come in many sizes."

This time, Matthew sat up in his seat with questions. "Do you farm right here?" he asked, pointing towards the water.

"Yes, close by, but we also have other areas in the bay that we use for three different size oysters," she answered.

"And where do you get your seeds from?" he asked.

Gladys smiled. "We actually run a hatchery in that building

over there," she explained, pointing to a building with metal siding behind the others. "We even have an on-site lab and technician to maintain quality control. That's a new position, but it has given us the credibility we needed." Glancing at Matthew in the rearview mirror, she said, "You seem to know a bit about oysters. Did you know that Lottie always talked about you, Matthew? She told me to keep my eyes on you for an oyster farm in Savannah."

Agnes felt the air leave her lungs and shivered in response. Lottie didn't know much about Matthew. But yet, she knew. The touch of Matthew's hand on hers made her jump. He gently squeezed before speaking.

"I barely knew Lottie. Why would she say such a thing?"

Gladys laughed. "There's a reason you're here. You might not see that yet, but there is. There always is."

He confusedly turned to Agnes, his eyes searching hers for an answer, but she only shrugged. Gladys interrupted his thoughts. "It looks like the gangs all here," she said as she pulled into a spot beside a building where several men were gathered. Some were in fishing gear, some were in wet suits, but many were in multiple combinations of both. They seemed to be waiting for her and were happy to see her.

As they exited the car, the men approached quickly. By the look on their faces, they were worried. They immediately began to ask her questions, but she raised her hand in response.

"This is my granddaughter Agnes and her friend Matthew from Savannah, Georgia."

This statement stunned them to silence, but they quickly found their words and welcomed them both. Then Gladys commented, "Let's all warm up inside and discuss the problem at hand."

Gladys led the way, and they all followed except Agnes and Matthew.

"What in the hell just happened?" Matthew asked. "Is she the boss here, too?"

"I really don't know. I'm still stunned that Lottie told her about you. I feel like we're actors in someone else's story, and I don't like it."

Matthew looked at her strangely, then slowly ran his hand up her arm, softly cupping his fingers around the back of her neck. His thumb rubbed under her chin line. "Don't worry, Agnes." She placed her hand on top of Matthew's at the same time he pulled her in for a kiss. It was the first time their kiss hadn't been full of passion. This time, it was full of trust. It was a kiss that made her realize that whatever came their way on this trip, they could handle it together.

"Are you ready to go watch your bad-ass grandma set all those men straight?" Matthew asked.

A huge smile moved across Agnes' face. "Let's go!"

The room buzzed with worry and energy, like a hornet's nest at spring's end. Agnes searched the room and found Gladys sitting at the table, slowly stirring her coffee while listening to the person on her left speak. She glanced up at Agnes and winked, motioning towards the coffee machine.

Matthew and Agnes snaked their way through the many conversations rolling around the room as they walked toward the coffee machine. Something made her focus on the industrial-sized kitchen just off the end of the room. *I should go make something*, she thought. *Oh my gosh, what am I thinking? Shake it off.* But a nagging feeling kept pulling her. *Lottie always had the ability to know what to cook at the right time, so this isn't completely absurd*, she reasoned. *Still, what would Gladys and Matthew think?* she asked herself. *They would think I was nuts if I walked into the kitchen in the middle of a crisis and started baking.* She surveyed the room. Everyone was nervously talking, trying to figure out a plan. They were scared. *Snickerdoodles. That's what they need. But I'm sure they don't have the ingredients.*

"Go look," came the voice in her head. So, she excused herself from Matthew and walked into the kitchen.

Shamelessly, she opened the refrigerator to find it well stocked, and the full box of butter and eggs were in date. *Okay, I've got the big stuff. I just hope they have the other ingredients.* Walking to the pantry, she was happy to find flour, sugar, baking powder, cinnamon, and cream of tartar. *Who keeps cream of tartar in a business kitchen*, she wondered. Grateful she had all the ingredients, she began to mix a quick batch of the sweet cookie. The men didn't notice anyone in the kitchen until they smelled cinnamon. By then, she was pulling the first batch of cookies out of the oven and carrying them to the coffee station.

When she returned with the second batch, she found a young woman holding the empty platter beside the table. "What were these?" she asked.

Agnes felt like a child being scolded and began to overexplain: "I have a café in Savannah, Georgia, and I've always loved to cook. So, when I saw that everyone seemed upset, I went into the kitchen and started baking."

"What were these, and why didn't I get one. That was what I wanted to ask," she said with a smile.

"Whew, I thought you were angry," Agnes remarked as she looked the young lady over. She seemed to be about her own age. She was tiny and cute, wearing a blue and white plaid flannel shirt, with her blonde hair pulled high into a ponytail. The word that popped into Agnes' mind was spitfire.

"Angry? Heck no. I smelled the cinnamon and followed my nose. I'm Tammy," she said, extending her hand. "I'm the cook here."

Agnes reached out and shook it. "You've got a great kitchen in there, Tammy."

Tammy stood a little taller with pride. "I couldn't agree more; I will try to take care of it. I haven't been doing this long. My mom was the chef for years, and I took over a few months ago. We are one big family here, so I always make a light morning breakfast and a hot lunch meal. This is the first time I've seen one of these emergency meetings. I didn't even think to make food, so thank you for jumping in."

"Honestly, it's the only way I feel I can help."

When the men noticed another batch of cookies, they trickled over to the table for seconds. The feeling in the room had changed. The raised voices had softened, and Agnes noticed a couple of men begin to laugh as they teased each other.

Tammy watched the men and then grabbed a cookie herself. Smiling, she leaned over to Agnes. "I sure could use some help with the food over the next couple of days."

Agnes agreed, happy to have a purpose. She felt the weight of someone staring and turned to find it was her grandmother. Gladys watched her intently. Although she smiled and nodded, showing her approval of her baking, there was a small wrinkle between her eyes. Curiosity? Concern? Agnes didn't know her well enough to read her expressions. But something had caused that crinkle across her brow, and Agnes was going to find out what.

34

FARM TO TABLE

The meeting lasted until dark, only ending when the foreman made his final decision. "We will begin to sink the baskets tomorrow. We cannot risk the ice growing so thick that we can't submerge them. Our whole crop could be lost. We'll have to take our chances at missing that last month of growth and let them go dormant early." Everyone nodded. He added, "Some of you may not know Patrick's wife, Gladys, very well. But we are so grateful that she came when she did. Thank you, Gladys, for explaining how it has been handled in the past. You are the only one who has seen this firsthand." The foreman paused a moment to let the men acknowledge Gladys. She smiled and nodded in response, then turned her attention back to the foreman who wrapped up the meeting, telling the group to go home and rest well for the day ahead.

Once the door shut, Gladys turned to Matthew. "We could use your help out there tomorrow. Could I tell the foreman you will help out?"

"I'd be honored to," Matthew answered.

Gladys nodded, "Good. I'll have Jake show you the ropes."

"What about me?" Agnes asked. "I want to help, too."

"I have you in the boat with me and Barry tomorrow, but I noticed you met Tammy earlier. Could you also work with her to get everything straight in the kitchen? She's new to the job and could probably use the extra help. You seem to know what people need to nourish their bodies." Gladys paused. "And their spirits. That's the best thing you can do when these boys are diving down under the ice." Gladys slowly pushed herself up from the table, holding on to it for balance. Agnes noticed her unsteadiness and went to her side. "It's been a long day," she said wearily. "And you haven't even met your grandfather yet. Unfortunately, he will be in bed by now. His nurse has him on farming hours, up with the sun and down at dusk. You'll get a chance to meet him soon, I promise. Now, help me into the house, and I'll show you to your room."

Gladys seemed to have aged twenty years from when they had pulled up at the oyster company. When Agnes went to her side, Gladys held on to her tightly. Matthew grabbed their luggage, and they began walking toward her home, the first house past the plant. It had turned dark outside, so Agnes couldn't get the lay of the land. But she could see the various houses that sat in a row past her grandmother's. They all faced the long dock that ran the stretch of the land. Many different types of boats were tied down its side. Vehicles and delivery trucks were parked along the property with the oyster company's logo.

"This place is huge," Agnes said as she and Gladys walked along slowly.

"It sure isn't the same place I came to many years ago. Things were so much simpler then. But, in truth, they were much harder, too. We never knew if we would make it from year to year. At least now we are more stable. But this early ice could definitely hurt us." She looked from Agnes to Matthew, realizing she hadn't informed them of the situation. "Our oysters run on a three-year cycle that depends on the weather. They progress from larvae to adult oysters. They grow for several weeks each year, between ice thaw and set-in. When either is off a few weeks, it throws the oysters off." She pointed to her mind. "Luckily, I have a good memory, and I remember the two other times this happened and what we did, so we should be fine."

They walked in the front door as Gladys finished her thought. "But there is a lot of work ahead."

"We're ready to help," Agnes announced, causing Gladys to turn to her. She cupped her hands around Agnes' face. "You will never know how happy I am that you're here," she said as she kissed Agnes' cheek. She then pointed down a long hallway. "Pick any rooms you'd like. They're all basically the same. We leave at sunlight. Goodnight," she said and walked off in the other direction.

Matthew watched her walk away and then turned to Agnes. "What is going on? I have so many questions, don't you?"

"Shhh," Agnes hissed, leading him down the long hallway. Gladys was right. All the rooms looked the same. "I wonder if this was an old fishing camp or something?"

"More questions," Matthew spit out. "Don't you want some answers? It's killing me."

Agnes shushed him again. "Let's get settled real quick. I need to pop back over and talk with Tammy about tomorrow. Then, I'll let you take me out to dinner," she added with a wink.

Matthew agreed. "Dinner and a drink. It's been a long day."

Within an hour, they returned to the main road and drove towards the town. There were several small places to stop for a meal, but they settled on a place called "Harveys." Agnes expected to walk into a restaurant with dark paneled walls and older furniture but was surprised by the off-white ship lap and comfortable pine tables. *Shame on me for assuming.* Following the hostess, they passed a large bar and a wall with many "vintage" maps and old black-and-white photos from the past.

"This place is charming," she said to Matthew, who agreed.

Once seated, the waiter brought their menus. On the top, it read "From Farm to Table" in large print. Under it, in a smaller font, it said, "Our farms are on land and at sea." She smiled and pointed to it on Matthew's menu. "Farms on the sea; that's a new concept."

Matthew agreed. "When we hear 'farm' in Georgia, we would never think it was on the water. But isn't that brilliant? Especially along our coast. We have so much land bordered by the Atlantic Ocean, and we eat from the sea; why wouldn't we farm it?"

"I couldn't agree more," Agnes answered as the waiter returned to the table to take their order.

They were happy when their meals came out quickly. Matthew raved about his pan-seared local halibut, commenting on how fresh the fish was. Agnes ordered fried scallops with a side of lobster mac-and-cheese. She didn't notice she had begun to bounce to the beat of music playing until Matthew pointed it out. She danced in her seat sometimes when she enjoyed what she was eating. But tonight, she was enjoying the songs being played, too.

Motioning to the bar area, Matthew commented, "He's pretty good. Want to stick around a little while and get an after-dinner drink?"

"I would love that. Let's find a cozy little table to listen to the music." They were disappointed to find all the small tables were full, so they found a seat at the bar. The people around them immediately welcomed them. They rarely had visitors, and they couldn't wait to learn more about them.

Agnes was happy when Tammy popped on the barstool right beside her. "You found the town hangout quickly," she said with a laugh.

"Yeah, and I beat you to it tonight," Agnes chided. Before long, they were laughing and talking like old friends. Matthew had also met people around him who were trying to educate him on the winning ice hockey teams that year. The sound of happy conversation circled the bar while everyone cheerfully listened to the music. When the singer announced the next song, he added, "This song goes out to all Canadians who defend their country, especially on Prince Edward Island. Let us take care of one another and realize that outsiders are just that, outsiders."

Matthew's face grew hard, but when he looked at Agnes, his anger quickly changed to worry.

35

THIS IS MY ISLAND

Matthew watched the bar patrons give one another questioning looks. "That was a weird intro to our song," Tammy said aloud.

Agnes turned to Matthew, whispering, "Was that directed at us?"

Matthew nodded. "I believe so."

"That was mean. Why would he say that?" she asked as she looked around the room in embarrassment. No eyes were on them, and everyone seemed oblivious to the insult.

As the song began, everyone sang along. Matthew and Agnes' new friends threw their arms around their shoulders and swayed back and forth. When the singer hit the chorus, the throngs of people around them joined. The bar was so loud that Agnes felt sorry for the restaurant patrons. But when Agnes looked around, everyone was smiling and swaying. Everyone except for her and Matthew.

When the song ended, the singer announced he was taking a break and headed toward the bar. Tammy hopped off her barstool as the singer approached, but he walked past her and straight to Agnes. Extending his hand, he said, "Hi. I'm Colin

O'Hara. I saw you at the plant today but never got a chance to meet you."

"Hi, Colin, I'm Agnes," she replied nervously.

"And I'm Matthew," Matthew said, thrusting his hand out, demanding attention.

Colin shook his hand and nodded but turned his attention back to Agnes. "You've been gone for a very long time. What brought you back to us now?"

The hurt in his voice stunned Agnes. *He knows me. But he sounds upset, like I hurt him. How could I have done that? I was just an infant,* she thought. The intensity of his stare silenced her as she searched the stranger's eyes for answers. The warmth of Matthew's arm as he wrapped it around her shoulder broke the moment. She welcomed his protective embrace.

Finally, Matthew spoke. "You offended us with your toast, and now you're questioning Agnes aggressively. What do you hope to accomplish here, mate?"

"My toast doesn't concern you." Colin paused for a split second, then added, "Mate."

"If it concerns Agnes, it concerns me," Matthew answered.

Colin reached for Agnes' hand, which was dangling from the side of the bar. He carefully lifted it, inspected it from side to side, and then gently released it onto the bar. "I don't see any wedding ring on that finger. Unless you do things differently in the States."

Agnes felt Matthew's tension and watched his chest begin to bow out. That one act made her find her voice. "You embarrassed us with your toast. It was rude. And I admit I have been gone for a long time. But I was adopted in the States and just found my grandmother last month. I had never even heard of Cavendish before that. Choices were made for me, not with me. I don't appreciate your speaking to me as if you know me. I can assure you that you do not. So, I'm saying goodnight to you. We have a long day tomorrow." She stood and walked toward the door, assuming Matthew was behind her. He was not. She turned just in time to see Colin fall to the floor, pulling two barstools down with him.

Colin jumped to his feet. He raced towards Matthew, ready to attack. The bartender watched the whole thing unfold. Jumping over the bar, he was between them in a split second. "Break it up," he yelled, trying to hold them apart.

Agnes ran to Matthew's side. Glancing over at Colin, she noticed Tammy holding onto his shirt. She nodded at Tammy, then followed Matthew out the door and straight to the car.

"I think you better drive," he said before opening the driver's side door for her. It wasn't until he was settled in beside him that she asked, "What in the world just happened?"

He only shook his head, so she asked again. "Matthew, what happened?"

"Just drive, Agnes. Please. Just drive."

Pulling out of the restaurant parking lot, her eyes bounced from the road to Matthew. *What made you push Colin?* she wondered. *It happened so quickly. Too quickly. What happened?* Agnes kept stealing glances at him, hoping he would start talking, but he didn't say a word until they were almost home. When the car turned down the gravel road, he could hold it in no longer.

"That smirk on Colin's face pissed me off. So I stopped in front of him and told him to stay away from you. He dropped his shoulder when I passed, so I turned and squared up with him. That's when he said, 'Mark my words; that girl will be staying in Cavendish.' It made me so angry I shoved him out of my way. I guess I shoved a little too hard. He hit the floor. I'm not sorry, though. I couldn't stand the way he acted towards you."

Agnes pulled in front of the house and parked the car. She reached out and took Matthew's hand. "Surely, this guy is delusional, but I want you to know two things. The first is that

Savannah is my home. I'm not sure what this alternate universe is or why we are in this craziness, but I know my family and home are in Savannah, and I have no intention of staying in Cavendish. Ever."

Matthew smiled and pulled her hand to his lips. "And what's the second thing?"

She tilted her head down, embarrassed to continue. "The second thing." She took a deep breath, mustering up courage. "I love you. I know we haven't dated long, but I do."

Matthew's grin went from ear to ear. He pulled her into him and kissed her deeply. Somewhere between kisses, he whispered, "I'm in love with you, too, Agnes." Then, he continued where he left off until they were interrupted by a knock on the door.

The plant foreman stood outside the driver's side window holding a flashlight. Agnes rolled down the window. "Can I help you with something?" she asked.

He growled, "Yes. You can help me get a good night's sleep. Can you go neck inside like normal people? Your foot is on your brake. The red brake light has flooded my bedroom for over thirty minutes now. I thought it was some teenagers out here smooching. I didn't know it was two adults."

The sting of embarrassment hit Agnes as if she'd been slapped in the face. "I'm sorry, sir. We are going inside right now," Agnes answered. She quickly rolled up her window while saying, "Oh my gosh, oh my gosh, I'm so embarrassed," under her breath as the man walked away.

"Maybe he's the one who needs to be embarrassed," Matthew said, pointing. The man's sleep pants had slipped low on his hip, exposing his bright white backside. A large anchor tattoo was penned across his right cheek. "Land Ho!" Matthew choked out, making Agnes laugh.

They giggled as they ran up the walkway into Gladys' house, but the cold turned the giggle into a shiver.

Once inside, her thoughts jumped to the men out on the water the following morning, especially Matthew. "Do you have the right clothes to be out in this weather tomorrow?"

"Yes," he answered with no uncertainty, then smiled. "Are you worried about me?" he teased.

"Maybe," she answered.

"How much?" he asked, opening the front door.

"Oh, just a tiny bit," she answered softly, trying not to wake anyone.

He held up his hand, showing how much a tiny bit looked between his thumb and index finger. "Just a tiny bit? Are you sure?" he teased and began to pinch her with those fingers.

"Yes," she giggled, trying to keep her voice down.

"Really?" he continued, backing her against the door jam. His teasing turned more serious. "Really?" he asked again.

She no longer giggled. She watched his mouth, waiting for it to make contact with hers. She whispered, "I feel like I've been punched in the gut. I'm so..." His mouth covered hers, leaving her sentence hanging in the air. And just like that, she forgot her worries and concerns. She was safe as long as she was in Matthew's arms.

36

MATCHING BIRTHDAYS

Agnes raced around the kitchen, trying to help Tammy finish breakfast before the group arrived. They had put on a pot of oatmeal, scrambled some eggs, and made yogurt cups with granola. When everything was complete, Tammy began preparations for lunch when she realized they were out of bread.

"I'm running to the store. Everything here is done except the coffee. I'll probably be back before the men come, but if not, just make sure they have what they need," she explained as she grabbed her keys and rushed out the door.

Agnes looked around the kitchen to ensure everything had been cleaned, then began brewing the coffee.

"What's your plans for your birthday?" came a voice from behind.

Agnes felt the chill run up her back. She recognized Colin's voice and whipped around to face him. "Who do you think you are coming in here like nothing happened last night?"

Colin held up his hands innocently. "I don't mean any trouble," he mumbled.

"Could have fooled me. Please leave me alone."

"Don't be mad at me; I didn't push anyone to the floor last night. I only want to talk with you," Colin replied.

She tried to steady herself. "You don't talk to someone by creeping up behind them and asking their plans for their birthday. How do you even know when my birthday is?" The weight of his stare was unnerving. Still, she held firm. *Don't break contact,* she told herself. *That gives him power over you.*

His eyes didn't move from hers as he walked further into the kitchen. "I know you," he whispered. "Whether you like it or not, we are connected. I was there the morning you were born." He pulled out a chair and sat at one of the many rectangular tables. "It was my birthday, too. I was eight and had seen my birthday cake sitting on the kitchen counter the night before. I was so excited about my birthday and couldn't sleep, so I snuck in the kitchen early, before everyone had awakened to get a lick of icing off my cake—the cake your mom had made for me. She was standing in the middle of the kitchen, drinking a glass of milk. I thought it odd for her to be standing so still until I looked down at the pool of water. She asked me to get your dad, and you were born that afternoon."

Agnes hadn't realized she had been holding her breath until he was finished. Taking a deep breath, she forced a smile, trying to hide her emotions. Softly, she whispered, "We share birthdays?"

"Yes, we do." A small smile crossed his lips, but his eyes brimmed with sorrow. "Your mom was a wonderful lady."

Agnes' emotions betrayed her. As much as she wanted to run from the room, the desire to know about her mom overtook her. She walked to the table and sat in the chair beside him. "What happened to my mom, Colin?"

"She passed away two weeks later," he answered. "They say it was an aneurism."

His brief sentence hit her like a slap in the face as she let the information settle into her brain. Her eyes began to fill with tears. *Please don't cry. Don't cry in front of this stranger,* she told herself. But they didn't obey. She felt the tear trickle down her face and quickly wiped it away, knowing she had to find out the rest of the story. Taking a deep breath, she asked, "And my dad?"

"He died in an accident a few weeks later. He was grieving and was careless on the water," he answered quickly.

She noticed Colin's discomfort as his eyes awkwardly bounced around the kitchen. He seemed to cringe when she began to cry and scooted his chair back from the table. "I know you need answers. I'm sorry for my bluntness," he said, awkwardly pulling his chair back towards her. Picking up a napkin from the table, he tucked it into her hand.

"What happened to me?" she managed to croak out.

His voice was barely audible as it came out in a hoarse whisper, "You disappeared."

Matthew walked in to find Agnes sobbing. Colin was sitting beside her with his arm pulling her close to his side. Matthew crossed the kitchen in two long strides and pulled Colin out of the chair and into the air.

"NO!" Agnes yelled. "No, Matthew. I'm fine. We're just talking."

Matthew was bewildered. "You don't look fine," he spit out. He slowly loosened his grip while not moving his eyes off Colin. "What did you say to her? Can't you see you've upset her?"

"That was not my intention," Colin said aloud. He turned his attention to Agnes. "I'm very sorry if I upset you, Agnes. But you deserve to know the truth." Turning to leave, he locked eyes with Matthew. "There are forces in play here that you are not aware of. I only want what's best for Agnes."

"Let me be the judge of what's best for Agnes," Matthew replied, sitting in the chair that Colin had just vacated. Agnes jumped into his arms. He held her tight as she sobbed on his shoulder. Eventually, they heard the swish of the kitchen door closing behind him.

When Agnes finally calmed down, she explained her conversation with Colin. "It's just so sad. This young couple had the world in front of them. And within weeks, they both were gone and so was their baby." She shook her head in disbelief. "I mean, so was I. That's really weird, isn't it? Obviously, I don't remember any of this. And it breaks my heart for Gladys. But I don't long for something I never had. There's a connection, for sure. But like I told you last night, my home is in Savannah with my family."

Matthew watched her compose herself as she discussed the situation, and when she was done, he said, "You know we can leave at any time. We can find a ride back to Charlottetown and be back in Savannah by nightfall. You don't owe these people anything. As you say, your life is in Savannah. But if you need to play this thing out, I'm right here by your side." He leaned over and kissed her forehead.

Agnes opened her mouth to speak but was interrupted by the group of workers coming in the door. She jumped up, told the group hello, and then explained the available food options. After everyone was served, she did what she always did—she moved to the side of the room to watch. She had learned to read people from a distance, so she studied each of them.

The workers moved about the room, fixing their plates and drinking coffee. When the foreman arrived, he called them together, blessed the food, and addressed them.

"We have a long day ahead of us and will work until dark. We know we won't finish today, so don't make any rash decisions. There is a list on the back wall of where each crew will go. Work steadily and stay warm. We don't want any fingers frozen off again this year." The group around a particular table hit one man on the back, making it obvious who was the past victim of the frost. "Now fill your bellies; we leave in twenty."

There was a buzz in the room, but unlike the day before, there was no worry. Decisions had been made, and now they were to be executed. No one seemed nervous or upset; they just chatted idly. It reminded Agnes of her family around the dinner table. She wondered how many of the workers were actually related and how many of them knew about her.

Matthew had found his name on the list but had no idea what "Boat 6/Bay" meant. He was happy when the captain of the crew introduced himself and explained. "We've got the easy job today in the bay. We will each wear waders and walk along the shallow water. We should be able to follow the ropes to pull each basket. Just make sure you keep all skin items waterproof, and you should be fine. Welcome to our crew and thank you for helping us."

Matthew noticed the men begin to file out one by one, but he wanted to tell Agnes goodbye first. "I'm going out to sea. Have you got a kiss for this old sailor?"

Agnes stood and gave him a quick kiss. "Please be careful. I really like all your fingers."

"I promise to come back with all ten," he answered. When he noticed the captain walking towards the door, he grabbed his jacket, gave her one last kiss, and quickly followed.

Agnes glanced around the room to find Colin watching her. He nodded, then made his way to the door, too. Once the room was empty, she smiled. The workers left happy with full bellies, and she had learned a little about each person, including Colin.

37

OFF TO SEA

Colin tried his very best not to stare at Agnes through breakfast. In fact, once he made his plate, he sat with his back to her. But after everyone was seated, she walked around the room and was now leaning on the wall directly in front of him.

She looks just like her mother, he thought, shaking his head. But once again, he had to remind himself that she had no idea what she had missed. She didn't know how her father had loved Colin and taken him under his wing. She didn't know the wonderful people their community had lost. She didn't know what it felt like to be hugged by her mother and father or how they had planned to adopt him. And she didn't know that his whole world had changed that one morning, the morning of their birthdays.

He kept his eyes focused on his plate. It would be a long day ahead, and he knew much of the decision-making would fall on his shoulders. Papa Pat had been slowly turning the company over to him, but he still doubted his ability to do the job. He was happy Gladys had kept the foreman in place after

Papa's collapse last year. Still, he had to make all the decisions. The livelihood of many people depended on it.

He finished his breakfast and stood to throw away his plate. Making sure Agnes was still in the room, he walked toward the kitchen to say hello to Tammy. Not knowing Agnes was helping Tammy in the kitchen had caused him a very emotional conversation earlier that morning. He hadn't been ready to have that conversation, but he wasn't sorry it had happened. He had told her the truth, and she deserved to know.

He was upset when Tammy was still not in the kitchen. Their mornings together had become something he looked forward to. But this wasn't an average morning, and tensions were high. He was sure Tammy was feeling nervous, too. Walking back into the dining room, he looked for Gladys, but instead, his eyes met Matthew's. He seemed like a nice enough bloke, and undoubtedly, he loved Agnes, but he was an outsider and would never fit in. Agnes did fit in. This was her home, and Colin was incredibly happy she had found her way back. He nodded at Matthew and kept scanning the room until he found Gladys.

She was sitting at a side table nursing a bowl of oatmeal. She looked so tired. A few months ago, she had called to tell him she wanted to move Papa Pat to Charlottetown into an assisted living facility where he would be closer to her. But that was before she went to Savannah to find Agnes. Now that she had brought Agnes home to help, Gladys may be around more.

He walked over to her table and sat down beside her. "How are you this morning?" he asked in a hushed voice.

Gladys smiled up at him. "I'm fine, Colin."

"Your hands say otherwise," he whispered.

Gladys glanced down to see her fork shaking in mid-air and quickly set it down. She grabbed her right hand by her left and rubbed it gently. "You know how the cold bothers the nerves in my hand."

He nodded with a smirk.

"I see that look on your face. I'm not sick; it's just been a long couple of weeks."

Colin answered, "I know it has. Will you be okay in the boat today?"

"Yes, thank you," Gladys replied.

Colin nodded toward the foreman, who called everyone to attention.

"Okay, men, let's begin by thanking Agnes for this great breakfast this morning." The group called out their thanks, and then he continued. "Let's pray." Everybody got to their feet quickly and bowed their heads. In unison, they prayed:

"Saint Brendan, patron saint of sailors,
    Guide us through the vastness of the sea,
    Protect us from storms and danger,
    Lead us safely to our destination.
    In your footsteps, we find courage and faith,
    May your intercession bring us peace and hope.
    Through Christ our Lord, Amen."

As soon as the prayer ended, the foreman announced, "We have a difficult task ahead, but we all know the ropes. Stay focused and watch out for one another. Godspeed."

Before walking out the door, the men looked at the large dry-erase board one last time, verifying the crew they would be working with. Colin waited for the last person to leave in case anyone had questions, then went to the door. He looked back just in time to see Agnes and Gladys laughing with one another. The image stopped him dead in his tracks.

In all his years of knowing Gladys, he had never seen her look like that. She almost looked like a different person, younger and happier. Confusion ran through him. Had Gladys been sad all these years, and he never noticed it? He always thought she was just a serious person. They would joke around with each other, but she always seemed dry and borderline cold. The Gladys in front of him was someone he didn't recognize. He continued to stare at the woman who had basically raised him. Had Agnes brought her this much joy in such a short time? And, if so, what would happen if Agnes left?

He hadn't realized Agnes had caught him watching them until it was too late. He nodded quickly, opened the door, and left. The frigid wind immediately hit his face, jolting him back to the present. He couldn't be distracted today. That's when accidents happen on the water when a person's mind wanders from the task at hand.

He was the last one on his boat. He wouldn't be working with a crew today; he would be hopping around, making sure everyone was safe and on task. He motioned to the first boat to shove off, then started his engine and waited for them each to make way. All six boats followed each other under the Cavendish Road Bridge and into the bay, then went in different directions.

The first two boats traveled the furthest. They had divers who would be securing the baskets of mature oysters on the bottom. Boats three and four were going to sites with shallower water, which required wet suits but no divers. They would be sinking the baskets into deeper water below the point where any water may freeze. The last two boats stayed in protected areas near the plant. They would be collecting first-year oysters that could not withstand the stress of the temperatures. These oysters were being brought back to be supervised while in cold storage.

They each carried different dangers, but everyone understood that the boats with divers carried the greatest. They all prayed the initial reports that the ice hadn't completely formed were accurate. The safety of every man was at stake. Each boat signaled as it broke rank, turning toward its intended destination. The people on the other boats waved as they left the family one by one. That's what they were to each other, family. Each person took care of the next, on and off the water.

38

COMING HOME

Agnes and Tammy bantered back and forth as they cleaned up breakfast. Agnes was surprised at how well they got along and enjoyed their time together. Gladys walked in just as they finished wiping down the counters.

"We have a busy day today, but a little time right now. Would you like to go and meet your grandfather?" she asked.

Agnes excitedly agreed, so she put on her coat and met Gladys at the door. The two women made their way down the sidewalk, which connected all the houses to the plant. When they entered through the front door this time, they turned left. The house seemed to run on and on. In addition to the many bedrooms down the hall on the other side, this side held the larger dining area and living room with several couches and recliners.

Gladys noticed Agnes looking about and explained. "This building was the old fish camp. Most of the men were unmarried, so they would live here. The married ones would rent out one of the houses along the docks. Over the years, things changed, and now several of the workers live around the

Cavendish area and drive to work. Only a couple of people still live in this house, but all the cottages are full. I know it's not extravagant by any means, but it's home and all we need.

Agnes smiled. The place was not extravagant, but it was kept tidy and comfortable. She could almost picture it full of men who had been on the water all day. "I bet it was crazy back in the days when all the rooms were full."

Gladys' eyes drifted to the main sitting area. Although she hadn't been around lately, she could remember when it was packed full. "You have no idea. There was so much energy when everyone was together. Now it's just so quiet."

They continued walking. Just past the kitchen was a small hallway that split into two rooms. One door was closed, but the other was propped open. The sound of a game show traveled across the room. Gladys announced herself over the loud television. "Hello? I've brought a visitor."

As they rounded the corner, they found the nurse sitting in one of two matching armchairs, watching the television. She quickly hopped up and turned it off. "Oh. Hello, Miss Gladys. I wasn't expecting you this morning."

"Good morning," Gladys answered curtly. She noticed her husband sitting in his wheelchair in front of the window, looking out over the docks. This was the place he liked the most. Gladys knew he had been on those docks every morning of his life, so it made sense. She reached out her hand to Agnes and pulled her into his vision. "This is our granddaughter, Agnes," she announced.

Agnes looked into his blank face, still staring out to sea, although she now blocked the way. She knelt in front of him and took his hand. His fingers curled around hers in response. "Hello," she said in the most casual voice she could muster.

His eyes focused on hers. "Maria!" he announced as a smile spread across his face.

Gladys was stunned. He had gone almost six weeks without

saying a word. The doctors had told her it was the disease finally taking its course. But here he was, calling out to his daughter-in-law, who had died so many years ago. There was no sadness this time; his face was full of joy. The same joy he had when his son had married that smart, young girl. Wasn't it a blessing to have all that sadness removed? Gladys envied him for a brief second.

He repeated her name, "Maria," and tightened his grip.

Agnes looked to Gladys, wondering what to do. But Gladys shook her head. "You can sit with him for a moment if you'd like, but he no longer understands," she said before finding her way over to one of the armchairs and collapsing into it.

Agnes began talking, the words dripping out. "I'm Agnes. You don't know me, but I'm your granddaughter. I'm so happy to meet you. I'm sorry I didn't get to you sooner when you could take me out to see the oysters. But I'll think about you today when I'm on the water and come see you when I return. I hope you have a great day." She then kissed his hand and stood to leave. He didn't let go. She looked down at him and noticed a tear running down his face, so she squatted back down by his side. "I'll be back, okay?" she said.

"Be safe, Agnes," he answered.

Those three words brought the nurse over in a split second, followed by Gladys, who leaned over to listen further.

Patrick's eyes traveled up to Gladys. "Agnes?" he uttered.

Gladys cupped her hands around his and Agnes' hands and answered, "Yes, Agnes. She's come home."

His clarity drifted just as quickly as it had come, and his hands slipped open from their grip. His focus returned to the window behind them, staring through them as if they weren't there.

"What just happened?" Agnes asked. "Did he hear me?"

"Yes," Gladys answered, still in shock he had connected with anyone, knowing there was no way he'd remember. "Yes,

Agnes. He did hear you, and he understood." She looked at Agnes, who still knelt at her husband's side. She did look so much like her mother, Maria. Things would have been so different if she were still alive. Agnes would have grown up on Cavendish, taking many boat rides with her grandfather. And she would still have her son.

39

MAKING THEIR ROUNDS

Their boat moved from spot to spot, bringing the soup, sandwiches, and coffee that she and Tammy had prepared to the different crews of men. They also brought wool blankets, fresh gloves, and towels. Everyone was grateful for their supplies and hot meals. The crews continued to work while the men made their way to Barry's boat one at a time. There was a job to be done and only so many hours of daylight, so they couldn't break for lunch as a group. This is when Agnes got to know the men. They loved sharing their stories while they gulped down their meal. Each one remembered that Patrick's wife, Gladys, had been a nurse, even if she hadn't been around in years. Each one began to ask her about their ailments, everything from indigestion to a wart on their hands. Agnes smiled as each one approached Gladys, surprised how the big, burly men would change their whole demeanor when they had questions for a nurse.

On their last trip, they took supplies to the boat where Matthew worked. Agnes watched him intently; he was in his element. He moved with ease in the water. He knew how to handle the oysters and hummed a song Agnes had never heard. Wading over to her boat, Agnes asked, "You having fun?"

His face got serious, "This is dangerous work, Agnes." Then he let his smile creep on his face. Leaning in, he whispered, "And I love it."

"Your secret is safe with me," she answered with a wink as he returned to the job at hand.

Agnes found her seat in the boat next to Gladys. As they pulled away, Gladys motioned back to Matthew. "That boy has the itch. I've seen it before, and they turn out to be amazing oyster farmers."

Agnes watched Matthew as the boat pulled away until he eventually fell out of sight. He did seem happy and excited. She had only seen him like that one other time, and that was the day he showed her the oysters near her house. Her mind began to spin. Could oysters be raised in baskets like this in Savannah? She pictured the spot and then pictured Matthew in it. Her mind shifted to the thought of Lottie on the bank watching him. "She knew," Agnes muttered, thankful for the roar of the boat motor. Once again, she was baffled that Lottie had noticed his abilities as a boy. She was deep in thought as the boat idled in the river before being maneuvered into the dock slip.

As they walked up the dock toward the house, Agnes announced, "I'm going to help Tammy warm up the soups and make fresh coffee for when the crews come in. Why don't you go and rest for a few minutes?"

Gladys pulled Agnes to a stop. Turning her towards her, she cupped Agnes' face into her hands. "You don't have to worry about me; I always take care of myself."

"I know that. But you can't expect me not to worry. I just found you, and I want to make sure you stay well," Agnes responded.

Gladys pulled her face in and kissed her on the cheek. "I

think I will take you up on that nap. Once all the crews come in, they will have a meeting. I'll be back for that."

"Sounds like a plan," Agnes answered, then helped Gladys back to the house. She realized Gladys was leaning on her much more than expected, so she helped her get inside and walked her to her bedroom. As Agnes left, she decided to check in on her grandfather across the hall. This time, she found him asleep in bed with the nurse reading a book in the corner. She closed it quickly as Agnes entered the room.

"He's been asking for you," the nurse said. "Actually, he's been asking for you and Colin."

"Me and Colin? Why?"

"I guess he wanted his family," she said matter-of-factly.

Agnes nodded at the nurse and thanked her before walking to the side of the bed. She felt a little guilty about intruding in his private moment of sleep, but she watched him intently, trying to memorize his features. The rhythmic sound of air being sucked in and let out, the rise and fall of his chest, connected her to him. She knelt beside the bed and stared at his face, trying to imagine how it may have once looked. But the nurse's statement haunted her thoughts. "I guess he wanted his family," she had said. He was her birth father's father. His blood ran through her. And yet, she didn't share any resemblance with him. She didn't have his nose, his eyes, or any of his features. Her mother's Hispanic traits must have overpowered them. Her mother. That was the first time she had called her that. She had always been very specific with the terms she used to separate her mother and birth mother, but somehow, they had morphed into one maternal figure. She would never know her birth mother but somehow felt her love through her adopted mother. She smiled as an image of the two women standing side-by-side flooded her mind.

Her eyes moved to the man in the bed as she tried to work through her feelings. *Why did you let me go? If I had just lost my son and daughter-in-law, I would have held on to their child with all my might. But you let me go.*

She leaned her head onto the side of the bed. She was so tired that her thoughts betrayed her and put her in turmoil. Was it better when she didn't know? She had a happy childhood, the best. She was always loved unconditionally. She had viewed her adoption as the way God brought her to the family she was supposed to be with. Why had Gladys come? Why had these feelings of not being wanted suddenly entered her world? She just wanted to go back. Back in time. Back to Savannah. Back to safety.

She felt a hand on her shoulder, but it didn't startle her. She slowly lifted her head, still lost in the daze of her thoughts, and turned into Colin's concerned face. She didn't shy away from him or think of anything witty to say. She also didn't try to remove his hand from her shoulder. As she began to stand, he extended his arms, and she fell into a strong hug.

The sound of her sobs filled the room, but Colin held her until she calmed down. "We are his family," she whispered.

He slowly let her go and stepped back. "Yes, we are. But you are his bloodline."

Noticing the movement in the bed, she turned to see her grandfather watching them. Worry covered his face, but he didn't utter one word. He searched the room, looking for someone or something. Then he began to grunt, flailing his arms back and forth in despair. The nurse was quickly at his side, injecting him with a shot. She counted slowly, "One, two, three." He began to calm. "Four, five." He relaxed. And on six, he was out.

40

THE FAMILY BLOODLINE

Colin and Agnes exited out the back door and began to walk a path leading away from the house. Seeing her grandfather's distress had been upsetting, so Colin suggested getting some fresh air before dinner.

"Where are we walking to?" she asked.

"I want to show you something. It's not far," he answered.

They walked a bit further before Agnes began, "I'm sorry you found me in such a mess. I'm usually not like this."

"You never have to apologize for being human. You've had a lot dropped on you at once," he responded.

"I just don't know where I fit into all this." She motioned with her hands to everything around her before turning her hands into a question.

"Funny you should ask," he said as they approached a small cemetery. "I know this may seem odd, but I thought you could see it better this way. This is the cemetery dedicated to the oyster company." He walked into it a little further and pointed to a section enclosed with an open iron fence. "And this is the family section." They stepped inside and walked down the path that led to the back. "These are the first O'Haras. The two brothers, James and William, were immigrants straight from Ireland."

Agnes looked at the tombstones and their dates of birth and death. The carvings were worn and barely visible, but she could see that one of the men died in January of 1842 and the other in September of the same year. Colin slowly continued walking. "And their children," he motioned to the side. "And their children's children. And it goes on and on."

Agnes followed along until he stopped in front of two of the newest headstones. One read "Henri Benjamin O'Hara," and the other was "Maria Diaz O'Hara." Agnes' stomach clinched. She had listened to every story about her birthparents, but seeing their tombstones physically hurt her, like a knife right in her gut. She felt drawn toward them, the genetic pull bringing her as close as humanly possible. She unknowingly had placed distance between herself and them, but now they were right in front of her. She had to connect with them. She had to verify that they had loved each other and that she was a product of their love. Pulling off her gloves, she placed a hand on each headstone. The freezing granite felt as if it were burning, but she held firm. Closing her eyes, she connected in silence. "I am fine. I was raised by a family who loves me, and I am happy. Thank you for having me. Thank you for loving me. I'm sorry I never got to meet you, but I hope we will be together again one day. Until then, know that I love you."

When she opened her eyes, Colin was watching her. Finding her voice, she began, "Eternal rest grant unto them, O Lord." Colin joined in, "And let perpetual light shine upon them. May they rest in peace." She made the Sign of the Cross and noticed when he did the same.

Colin didn't try to hide the fact that he was staring.

"What's wrong?" she asked.

He shook his head and almost didn't answer. But after a brief pause, he replied, "It's just the image of you standing between the graves of your parents and saying a prayer over them. I can honestly say it's something I never thought I would see. I know it sounds weird, but it makes me happy." He backed away from the graves, then turned and wiped his eyes before walking out of the fenced section.

Agnes wandered around the tombstones, looking at the names and dates. When she finished, she met Colin at the gate where he was waiting. He motioned to the O'Hara name on the top of the fence. "These are your people, Agnes. You are one of them, and you belong in Cavendish."

The strangest feeling hit her as she glanced up at the name on the gate. She couldn't place it for a second but soon acknowledged it as pride. She was proud to have come from this family. They were strong and dedicated. They worked hard and leaned on one another. However, she had no intention of moving to Cavendish. *Should I tell Colin I won't be staying, or would that sound rude?* She wondered.

The moment passed as Colin walked out of the cemetery, and she quickly followed behind. She was surprised when Colin turned away from the house, continuing further down the path they had begun. It was bitter cold, but the thick woods blocked the wind. The rhythmic sound of the hard earth crunching beneath her shoes suddenly made her aware of her surroundings. She looked up into the high trees, almost bare for the winter. Breathing in, she filled her lungs with the smell of pine mingled with salt water. *This really is a perfect setting*, she thought to herself.

"Isn't it beautiful?" Colin asked, almost as if he had read her mind.

"It's amazing. What a perfect place to grow up," she answered.

He nodded with a half-smile but didn't reply. *What is he thinking?* she wondered as the path began to ascend. The hard soil beneath her slowly turned into crushed red rocks as the smell of salt water became stronger. They had walked away from the docks, so she was disoriented. They continued walking toward an opening in the distance.

Her mind replayed Colin's words in the cemetery, "You belong here." He had emphasized the word "you". But her grandfather's nurse called them family. Colin had mentioned that he wasn't blood-related, but his last name was O'Hara. She was about to ask him questions as they hit the clearing. "Wow!" she exclaimed. "What is this?"

He chuckled, "These are cliffs."

"Well, I know that," she said, rolling her eyes. She walked to the edge and looked down over the red rocks and into the water about fifteen feet down. Her eyes traveled down the coastline, where the cliffs grew higher and higher, then looked down the other direction to where they ended in the ocean. "This is beautiful," she muttered, looking for Colin, who had found a seat on a massive red boulder.

"These are the red sandstone Cliffs of O'Hara," he said with a wink, then motioned down the coast. "Those are the Cavendish Cliffs, part of Prince Edward Island's National Park. They begin right past our land."

"I love it here," she announced as a gust of freezing wind hit her in the face. She struggled to catch her breath, then added, "But I'd like to see it when it's warmer outside."

"You'll have plenty of time," Colin replied. Looking into the sky, he added, "Now, let's get home." When they turned to re-enter the path, she noticed the clouds. "Snow's coming, probably before we get back to the house," he said. "Can you walk faster?"

Agnes thought back to all those team runs in the snow in Indiana. "Are you kidding me? Let's run." His smirk challenged her, making her want to sprint. Still, she knew she had to start slow, so she began to jog.

"Oh, you were serious?" he called out, but his voice mingled with the wind.

She grinned and continued to run, not bothering to look back. She found her pace and ran strong. When she came to the cemetery, she thought, *I'll just wait for him here.* She slowed, and he flew right past her. She had to stop and laugh when she noticed he was still wearing his hiking boots.

"Try to keep up," he yelled over his shoulder.

She caught up quickly and fell in behind him. Running with Colin reminded her of her brothers. They always pushed her to be strong, never underestimating her abilities. That's how this felt with Colin, and she liked it. They ran until the house came into sight, and then he slowed to a walk.

"We never would have made it if I hadn't taken the lead," he teased.

"Yeah, you saved us both," she replied, still trying to catch her breath. As they walked the rest of the way to the house, she noticed how it seemed different between them now; they both were at ease. *This is the best time to talk*, she thought. So, she jumped right in. "So, Colin. When you told me the story about turning eight and wandering in the kitchen early in the morning, it sounded like you lived here. Did you?"

"Yeah, I did," he answered curtly.

"So, how are we family? What gives?"

Looking down to the walkway, he kicked a pinecone off the path. "My father worked at the oyster company. We were vagabonds and the O'Haras were nice enough to hire him and take me on, too. My father died when I was seven. Truth be known, I don't remember much about him. But I remember everything about your father. And your mother, too." He turned to look at Agnes. "They were amazing, Agnes. They lived at the camp, in the back suite, and took care of me. They were actually in the process of adopting me when they died." He shook his head and then paused to clear his throat. "After a couple of years, Gladys and Patrick took over the paperwork and adopted me when I was ten."

"Then that makes us—siblings? Or are you my uncle?" she asked. "It feels a little like a soap opera."

He bristled. "Maybe a little, but this is my life. Unfortunately, I'm not their bloodline; you are," he answered.

She knew he had just given her the ammunition she needed. "They adopted you. That makes you their bloodline."

Colin stopped walking. "I don't think it works like that."

"Of course it does, just like in the Bible. Whenever my brothers or I had questions about our adoptions, my dad would tell us how Joseph adopted Jesus, which made him Joseph's heir and a son of David. Families give a child their name through adoption. Who are we to question the Holy Family?"

His laugh startled her. "Think about what you said a minute ago. We are like a soap opera. We are definitely not the Holy Family. The couple that I thought would be my parents died. The man who raised me has lost his marbles. The only woman I had as a mother figure was always MIA. And now she shows up with the baby, which I was forced to forget about years and years ago. Well, let me tell you one thing, we are the most unconventional, pieced-together family ever."

Agnes took a step back, giving him room to vent. "Whoa! How do you really feel?"

The sound of the backdoor slamming got their attention, and they turned to see Matthew standing on the porch with his arms crossed.

"Why in the world would you bring your boyfriend with you to meet your family for the first time?" he said under his breath.

"Because I was unsure what I was getting into," she said between clenched teeth. "And after that little temper tantrum, I see that I made the right choice."

Colin only snickered, then walked away.

41

SNOWED IN

The snow came hard that afternoon, quickly covering the docks in a blanket of white. Agnes watched from the window as each crew came in from their jobs. One by one, the men ate and drank, trying to warm their bellies while renourishing their bodies. They talked among themselves, proud of their accomplishments for the day. Each man's happiness grew larger after each story and each drink. All except for one man, Colin.

Colin paced the dock, constantly talking into a handheld radio, trying to get in touch with the only boat still out, Boat 1. He knew that particular crew had dangerous work, so he had stacked it with his most knowledgeable and hardest workers. Still, he worried. They were the last crew he had checked on before returning to the house. They had been waiting for the last diver to surface before returning to shore. Surely, something went wrong. He had been back for over an hour and had spent that time showing Agnes the cemetery. *I let my guard down*, he thought, cursing himself for letting life distract him.

I can't wait any longer. He ran to the shed for equipment and keys and hopped in the small boat. As soon as he cranked the engine, he saw the crew coming around the corner. Jumping from the boat, he motioned to the men who gave the thumbs-up sign. Feeling his shoulders ease, he cleared the dock for them to disembark.

The men were covered in snow and ice, but each one seemed fine as they quickly began to put their gear away so they could get inside the warm building. The foreman yelled over the sound of the icy wind, "There was an accident, and we stopped to help. One of the O'Brien's boats turned over at the point. They are still searching for one man, but it's been over an hour." The foreman made the Sign of the Cross, praying for the seaman who had been lost.

"Go warm up inside; I'll handle the rest," Colin ordered. The foreman nodded with respect and followed the command.

Colin began to clean the boat as much as possible in the freezing temperatures. Flushing the engines and scrubbing the hull was impossible with sleet and snow, but he did his best. As he cleaned, he thought of the O'Brien employee. *Just like Henri O'Hara*, Colin thought. He tried to shake off the image of his frozen body, but once you see something like that, you can never un-see it. Boating accidents were always horrible, but boating accidents as the ocean freezes were the worst. Bodies weren't found until after the thaw, and families hung in limbo for months. His heart went out to the family.

He was deep in thought as he cleaned, so he was surprised when someone stepped into the boat. As he looked up, he noticed Matthew had begun to clean the front. *I don't need his help*, he thought. *But then again, if he wants to help, who am I to tell him no?* They worked side by side until everything was cleaned and put away.

"I think we're done," Colin bellowed over the wind. "Let's get inside before we freeze to death." They burst through the mess hall doors with an explosion of wind and snow behind them. Everybody in the room went quiet but then roared in applause. Colin laughed, bowed, and motioned to Matthew, who did the same. Agnes approached with two shots of whiskey and handed one to each man, who turned them up quickly.

The foreman motioned for Colin to join him, leaving Matthew and Agnes alone. She shot him an angry look and fired off, "Why didn't you tell me you were doing that? I couldn't find you, and I panicked. I asked if anyone had seen you, and one man pointed outside. I have to say, I was shocked to see you helping Colin." Then she softened, "It was really nice of you."

"Wait. Are you mad or happy? I'm getting mixed signals, but both of them make me want to do this." He grabbed her around her waist, pulled her into his arms, and kissed her. It wasn't a kiss of passion or desire; it was the kiss of a man whose exhilaration had nowhere else to go. His lips were cold and clammy and tasted of salt water and sweat. Melted snow fell from his hair into her face, causing her to pull back.

Swatting him off, she chided, "Oh my gosh. You are disgusting!" then turned and walked away. The men around them laughed at the scene, knowing that each of them had lived a similar one.

"She loves me," Matthew said into the crowd, making everyone laugh harder and begin to tease him. He shrugged them off and laughed along until the melted ice began to drip down his back. He quickly pulled off his coat and wet layers of clothes and threw them in the drying room.

The sound of a shrieking whistle quieted the room.

The foreman said, "I have an announcement to make." Everyone gave him their full attention. "We did it! And it only took a day," he cried out.

The room roared with approval. He hushed everybody back down.

"It's been a long day, ye know? And the snow is coming

harder and harder. I wish we could celebrate longer, but we all best get home before we are stuck in this room for days. I love you each like brothers, but by day two, we would be swinging at each other." The men laughed, then quieted themselves. "I thank God above for keeping us all safe. Now go on home to your loved ones."

The men said their goodbyes, gathered their things, and obediently headed toward the door. Agnes was shocked by how quickly the room cleared and realized they knew how fast you could get trapped in the snow. She and Tammy cleaned off the tables and then went to the large pots on the stove, which were now empty. "Good gosh, those men can eat," she mumbled.

"Yes, they can," Gladys answered as she walked up behind her granddaughter. She placed her hand on her shoulder and said, "You did well today, Agnes, on your one and only day of work for the season."

Agnes smiled at the thought. When she had volunteered to help, she was scared she would be there for weeks. But it was over before it began. "I'm sure everyone would have been fine without me today, but I'm glad I could lend a hand."

"I know I couldn't have done it without you," Tammy shouted out over the sound of water running into the empty soup pot.

"Every job makes the company run. You took care of these men today and they know it," Gladys replied.

Agnes nodded, then turned back to the work in the kitchen. "Right now, my job is cleaning up this mess."

"We'll have it done quickly," Tammy called out.

Agnes walked over to where Tammy stood at the sink and turned the water off. "You need to get home before you're stuck here for days. I've got this."

"No way; there's too much to do," Tammy answered.

Gladys reiterated what Agnes said. "It'll get done. You really need to get home."

Tammy looked over at Agnes, who was nodding her head, and then agreed. She hugged both their necks, grabbed her coat, and ran out the door. Gladys watched her go and then picked up a rag to begin helping.

"Oh no, you won't. You were tired today, and I worry about you overdoing it. Why don't you return to the house and save me a seat in front of the fire?" Agnes suggested.

Gladys paused for a moment, looking at the mess in the kitchen and contemplating the situation.

"I worked cleaning up after long shifts for Lottie, I'll be fine," she remarked.

Gladys finally agreed. "I'll save you a seat right beside mine," she announced, setting the rag back onto the table. "But hurry up, the cider is hot."

Agnes immediately got busy. She felt her energy waning and knew she'd better finish before it all disappeared. Luckily, she had the skills for cleaning a restaurant that Lottie had taught her in high school. "Three S's. Soak. Scrub. Store everything away," she would say at the night's end.

Agnes thought about Lottie as she cleaned that night. Lottie had been to Cavendish. How in the world had she kept this secret from her? She didn't like this new feeling of animosity towards someone who had meant so much to her, but it had crept into her heart, and she struggled to expel it.

Thoughts. There were so many thoughts from throughout the day. Her body cleaned on autopilot as her mind tried to process the day's events. Colin. How did he fit into her world? Gladys and Patrick. She didn't even know where to begin with all her questions about them. Then there was Matthew. That smile on his face when he was on the water earlier and then when he came in from the boats. Her stomach tightened; would his smile always make her stomach do somersaults?

She looked around the room. One good thing about cleaning on autopilot is that you finish much faster. She was already on the last S, so she stored everything away, put on her coat, and turned off the lights.

The wind was so strong she could barely stand up. She covered her face and pulled her jacket snugly around her. Bending into the wind, she walked the short distance to the house. The warmth that hit her when she opened the door pulled her inside. But as soon as she shut the door, exhaustion set in. She stood motionless in the foyer, listening, but there was nothing but silence. Her mind slipped deeper into the fog that it was already fighting. *I've never been so tired,* she thought as she felt herself start to sway. She shuffled down the hallway, dropping her coat somewhere along the way, and tumbled into her bed.

42

DARKNESS AND LIGHT

Howling. Where was that sound coming from? Was she dreaming? Agnes shivered as she tried to wake herself up. *Where am I?* she wondered as she turned onto her side. Her feet were heavy, and she was wet. "What the hell?" she muttered. Opening one eye, she stared into the darkness as the howling sound returned. She pushed herself up and tried to wiggle her toes before realizing they were still inside her boots. Then she remembered walking in the front door and staggering down the hall.

Her eyes searched the room for the glow of a clock but couldn't find one. The room was pitch black. The only light was coming through the window. She stood, trying to find her balance, and walked toward it. When she opened the curtains, she stared out into darkness. The only thing visible was the white of the snow. Acknowledging the vast difference between the darkness and light, she peered deeper into the night but was once again disturbed by the howling sound. This time, she could pinpoint it. She ran her finger down the glass until it came to a small hole. She held her hand over it to feel the minuscule burst of air where the cold wind was trying to escape the freezing temperatures. Agnes recognized the shape of a BB hole from growing up with so many brothers. "I'm sure there's a great story behind this, but right now, I'm freezing," she muttered.

She felt her way slowly around the room until she found the light switch. But when she flipped it, nothing happened. *Is the power off?* she wondered, shivering once again. She felt her way back to the bed, grabbed the quilt, and wrapped it around her shoulders. Feeling her way across the room, she opened the door to darkness. Knowing the living room area was down to her left, she slowly moved her hand along the wall, pausing when her toe caught on something. Curiosity made her run her foot over it, but it didn't move. It felt like a blanket or a piece of clothing, so she pushed it to the side and continued. Her movements quickened when she noticed the flicker of light ahead. Once she entered the foyer, she realized it was firelight.

She found Gladys asleep in a recliner in front of the fire. But as she scanned the room, she noticed Matthew, Colin, and the foreman asleep in other chairs around the room. She stood still as she scanned her surroundings and saw the mantle clock, which read 5:05. Her eyes focused on the open recliner directly beside Gladys. She smiled, remembering Gladys' promise to Agnes that she would save it for her. So, she quietly sat down, snuggled into the quilt, and fell back asleep.

Agnes woke to someone rubbing the top of her hand. When she looked up, she realized it was Gladys.

"Good morning," Gladys said with a smile.

Agnes stretched her arms and groaned, "Good morning, Gladys." Her eyes scanned the room, noticing the empty chairs, then looked at the mantle clock. "Eight-thirty? How did I sleep until eight-thirty?"

"Rest is good, especially when you've worked so hard. Besides, we have nowhere to be today. We're snowed in. But the snowstorm seems to have ended. So, for now, we're going to just stay warm," Gladys answered.

Agnes pulled her quilt in tighter. "Staying warm sounds great. Do you know where Matthew and," she paused and changed her sentence, "and the guys went?"

"They got the generator for Patrick's room working last night, but the weather was so bad, I asked them to wait on the downstairs until today."

Agnes nodded and walked to the large picture window overlooking the water. "The world is so still," she said softly. "When it snowed at Notre Dame, people all over the campus seemed to enjoy it. But today, it's as if the world around us has disappeared." She glanced at Gladys, who was listening but didn't comment, so she turned back to the window and the sight beyond. There wasn't one footprint all the way to the water. Everything seemed so clean and fresh like a blank page just waiting to be written on.

Gladys' voice interrupted her thoughts. "The world around us has disappeared."

Agnes thought for a moment, then jumped in. "There will never be a more perfect time for us to talk." Gladys only nodded. "Can you tell me about Colin?"

The question hung in the air, so Agnes moved closer to Gladys and settled back into her recliner. Gladys cleared her throat and began. "Wexford Oyster Company has been operating since 1818. Two brothers, who were Irish immigrants, started the business. There are only two living family members left, Patrick and you. But many families have joined our team. For generations, we have hired an alliance of fishermen who were the best of the best. Others have wandered in, men and women who had been trying to operate oyster farms on their own or distant relatives needing work. But Colin's story was unique. His dad was a drifter and needed a job for the season. Colin was just a young boy when he came to the farm. His father knew nothing about oysters but was a hard worker, and we needed some muscle.

The company had hired drifters before, but none had ever shown up with a child. Still, we hired his father for the season, not knowing it would be his first and his last. When he got sick that January, he never got better. He left this world with three dollars in his pocket and a seven-year-old boy sleeping beside him in a twin bed."

"That's awful," Agnes interjected. "Poor Colin."

"Those were sad days, for sure. But he was so little, and there was always so much action around here. He always loved Henri the most. He followed him around constantly. Henri was in his early twenties, and he loved being with Colin. Before long, Henri met Maria. You would have thought Colin would have gotten lost in the shuffle, but instead, he was pulled into their mix. They acted like a little family. As soon as the two were married, they started the process of officially adopting Colin. In the meantime, they became pregnant. With you." Gladys reached out and took Agnes' hand.

"So, the adoption never went through?" Agnes asked.

"No, not for Henri and Maria. But once the adoption process had begun, the county had gotten involved. So, after they passed away, the county wanted to take Colin to a group home. Patrick didn't want to allow that, but I had my reservations. First of all, I knew I was old, and I was grieving, but most of all, I was worried about your future. I wanted you to have the company that you would have been given if your father had not died. So, I agreed with Patrick to adopt Colin, but I made him sign an agreement stating that the company would be passed to blood heirs only. That sounds harsh, but I had to look out for my own. After he signed and we were approved, we adopted Colin." Gladys realized Agnes was crying and wiped the tears away. "There, there. Colin turned out fine."

I'm not so sure Colin did turn out fine, Agnes thought, her bitterness surprising her. She adopted Colin, but yet she gave her own granddaughter up for adoption. It made no sense. She had to find a way to ask nicely. "You catch more flies with sugar than vinegar," she could hear Lottie saying. *I'm mad at you, too*, she thought, pushing Lottie from her mind.

Agnes decided to go around the back end of the conversation. "Colin said we shared the same birthday. How did he know me?"

Gladys looked surprised, but gradually, a smile moved across her lips. "Oh, yes. Colin knew you well. In fact..." Her sentence trailed off while she recalled a memory. Her eyes glazed, deep in thought. It was almost like she had gone back to that moment. "While we all grieved, Colin was the only person who could keep you from crying. Looking back on it now, I see he was way too young to be taking care of you. And he was grieving, too. But at the time, we lived minute to minute, then hour to hour, until we could finally make it through a full day." Gladys suddenly realized she was talking. She snuck a look at Agnes, who only stared in disbelief, then dropped her head. Defeated.

"Didn't you want me?" Agnes whispered.

Gladys sat up, her hand jumping to her chest. "You were always wanted. But when a sixty-something-year-old lady is given the task of mothering an infant, you have to wonder what kind of life the child would have. Colin was nine then and pretty self-sufficient, and Patrick was ill. We didn't have any other family. The day Lottie found me, she rescued you. When she mentioned a young family whose mom was actually my niece, with lots of brothers in Savannah, it just felt right. I remembered my happy childhood growing up in Savannah and wanted that for you, too. The only thing standing in your way was my selfishness. I was trying to hold on to my only tie with my son. I had to see for myself first. That's when I went to Savannah, only to discover that people were still looking for me. So, I agreed to Lottie's plan, knowing you'd have an amazing family, and I returned to my home here." She stopped and took a deep breath. "Not one day has passed that I haven't questioned my decision." She raised Agnes' hand to her lips and kissed it softly. "Can you ever forgive me?"

Agnes smiled through the pain in her heart and nodded slowly. "I'm not sure what my life would have been like if you had kept me and raised me in Cavendish, but I'll tell you this, I love my family, and I'm very blessed that you chose them for me." Her thoughts went to the mother who raised her, who loved her unconditionally, who would pull her onto her lap even though she was twenty-five years old and snuggle her just like she was three. She heard her voice before she thought about what she was saying. "I think I'm ready to go home." Gladys looked up quickly in surprise. "I'm so grateful you shared all this with me, but my home is in Savannah. The home you chose for me."

"I think we have a lot to discuss before you leave," Gladys replied, her voice changing to an almost business-like tone.

"I think we've said all that needs to be said—for now, at least," Agnes answered. But in case you need to hear this or you have any remorse, I want you to know that I forgive you. I have no ill feelings toward you, and I understand that you did what you thought was best."

Gladys nodded slightly, then added, "I think you need to be aware of one more thing."

Agnes took a deep breath. She didn't care to know any of the ins and outs of their business, but she sat quietly listening. She was happy to hear the door open and the footsteps of the men walking in from the kitchen. They would bring a distraction that would allow her to leave. Instead, Gladys kept talking. She would not be silenced. The men entered the room in a boom of excitement just in time to hear Gladys tell Agnes, "You own half of this company."

43

THE PLAN

The lights came on just in time to see Colin's face. His eyes cut like knives towards Gladys as he stood in the doorway.

Matthew crossed the room and stood directly in front of Agnes. Searching her eyes, he whispered, "Are you alright?" When she nodded, he slowly moved towards the window, but his eyes never left her.

The sound of the foreman murmuring caught everyone's attention. "Uh. I'm gonna go... there's a lot to be done. Okay. Bye."

The foreman's awkwardness made Agnes laugh out loud, but she was met by Colin's steel gaze. "I think I need to be in on this conversation. This is my future you're discussing."

Gladys said, "Let's talk about this over breakfast." She pulled herself out of the recliner and disappeared into the kitchen.

Colin immediately lashed out at Agnes. "Didn't you think I might want to hear all of this?"

"She was sharing my adoption story and blurted out that line at the very end. I'm glad you walked in to hear it yourself.

Why didn't you mention that little gem when we went for our walk yesterday?" she remarked.

Colin's eyes fell to the floor, then uttered, "I didn't know." He glanced toward the kitchen and added, "Maybe we should continue this conversation with the one person with the answers."

Agnes watched Colin leave the room. Turning to Matthew, she asked, "Will you stay with me?"

He only nodded once before Agnes grabbed his hand and pulled him towards the kitchen. Gladys was taking her first bite of hot oats when they entered. Agnes held back for a moment, watching her and Colin at the kitchen table, trying to assess what was going through each of their minds. Gladys just wanted out. She worried about her husband and wanted to move away from Cavendish. Colin loved the company and the men. This company was his life.

Matthew plopped down at the table. She smiled, picturing his happiness out with the oysters the day before. He didn't have a dog in this fight, but she knew how much he appreciated the business and valued his opinion. Agnes had zero knowledge of oyster farming. And if she was being completely honest with herself, she had no desire to find out. But she offered something no one else at the table did: She knew how to structure a business.

When she received her scholarship to play basketball at Notre Dame, she was asked to declare a major before accepting. She was unsure and had gone to her dad for advice. He had said, "Everybody needs a basic knowledge of business. You could be the greatest creator of juju bead necklaces, but you will fail if you don't know what to do with them." She took his advice and was surprised at how easily the concepts came to her. And in true Notre Dame form, they went over and above to submerge their students in challenging situations. She had attended many business conferences in Chicago, learning about real-life issues. She had studied companies that were dedicated to their employees and their families. She just needed to look at the oyster company without any personal prejudices.

The minute she sat down, all eyes turned to her. "I think there is a way to figure all this out where we all get what we want. You've got a profitable, well-organized company here with loyal employees and strong leaders." She looked to Colin, who smiled and nodded back to her. "Can you give me today and let me work on a few things? And Gladys, can you get me all the paperwork you have on the company, including the latest bank statements?"

"I sure can," Gladys said in between bites of breakfast.

"Colin, can you write out a five-year plan for the company? Areas that you feel where we can grow and areas that aren't working for us?"

"Oh yeah. That should be easy. I've got some great ideas," he answered.

"Perfect! Now let's eat; I'm starving." She rose from the table to find something for breakfast but stopped dead in her tracks. Slowly, she backed up to Matthew. Leaning over, she whispered. "Can we talk after breakfast? I've got an idea."

Agnes spent the rest of the day reading, organizing, and planning. She looked over every inch of the company and got everybody's input. But when she spread all the information across the table, she realized there was one piece of the puzzle still missing.

Walking into her grandfather's room, she found him staring out the window at the snow-covered boats. She knelt beside him and placed her warm hand on his ice-cold ones, but he didn't flinch. She squeezed a little harder, hoping to get a response. However, he remained in a trance, his mind locked in the past, trapped inside the shell of the man who had made such a solid impact on the people around him.

She sat on the ground beside him for a long time, looking out into the stillness of the cold. It was mesmerizing. Although the snow had stopped, the movement around the water kept her attention. At some point, she began to hum. She wasn't even sure of the tune, but when it started to take shape, it morphed into Amazing Grace, which surprised her. That wasn't one of the songs she had ever sung, yet she had begun to actively hum the tune. As her humming grew stronger, she felt the squeeze of her grandfather's hand. Although his eyes still focused on the water, his hand now held hers firmly.

She continued to hum as they both stared into the cold. It wasn't until she stopped that she felt him pump her hand twice in response. She pulled up a chair beside him and was surprised when his focus shifted to her face.

"Hello," she said quietly.

At first, he looked scared, but his expression quickly softened. His eyes searched hers. "You're not Maria," he whispered. "She passed away."

Agnes smiled. "No, I'm her daughter, Agnes. Your granddaughter."

A small tear moved slowly down his cheek. Agnes reached up and wiped it away.

"I'm sorry," he whispered as another tear fell.

"You have nothing to be sorry for."

"I do. I should have," he sputtered, "...tried harder... to keep you."

"You did what you could."

He nodded and looked out the window at the water. "You weren't here...but I worked hard for you...to have a company... to come back to. We owe you."

"Thank you, Granddaddy. I really appreciate your hard work. But if you wouldn't mind, I'd like Colin to take the reins."

He turned to look at her once again. "You look like your mother but have your daddy's heart. He was such a good boy." His voice broke, and he began to weep openly. Agnes scanned the room for a tissue and went to retrieve one. When she returned, he was again in his trance, staring out the window. The only thing left to prove the conversation had taken place were the tears still on his face. She wiped them dry, but he didn't respond. She then wrapped her hands around his, but the moment had passed. Still, there had been a moment. A single, unforgettable moment that set everything right in her world.

She processed everything he had just shared with her. He had seemed happy that Colin would run the company. But as soon as the grief over losing his son took over, he slipped back into the distant recesses of his mind. Maybe God was shielding him from his grief. She sat and stared with him until the setting sun darkened the room. Then she leaned over and kissed his forehead, saying, "I'm so happy you connected with me. You'll never know how much it helped. I love you."

44

HOMEBOUND

Matthew saw Agnes through the window as he approached the large mess hall. She sat at one of the long tables with papers and files spread around her. Shaking his head, he wondered how everyone around her had suddenly dropped everything in her lap. But things began to make sense as he continued to watch through the window. Agnes was undoubtedly brilliant, but it was more than that; she didn't need their help. Each of them was searching for something: a job, security, or even forgiveness. But Agnes was happy with or without any of this, which made her judgment clear.

"Where do I fit into all of this?" Matthew mumbled, quickly looking around to make sure no one heard him. He glanced back at her sitting at the table and watched her shift papers. Her hair fell into her face, and she pushed it out of her eyes. She must have seen his movement outside the window because her eyes moved his way. When she focused on his face, she smiled. He waved his hand, not taking his eyes off her. When she motioned for him to come inside, he moved toward the door but paused as his hand grabbed the doorknob. *I've been searching for something, too,* he thought as the door swung open.

"Hey, I've missed you," she called out as she wrapped her arms around him and pulled him inside.

He picked her up but stumbled through the doorway. "That wasn't exactly like I pictured it in my mind," he said with a laugh. But he was happy with the results when she continued to hold on to his neck and began kissing him.

She finally pulled back and blurted, "I'm ready to go home."

"Oh, are you now? It's 11:30 at night, fourteen degrees outside, and the roads are covered with snow," he answered. But when he saw the disappointment in her eyes, he knew he would do whatever it took to make her happy. "But we can figure all that out if you're serious." He was rewarded with a huge smile.

"Come here. I want to show you everything I found."

He followed her to the table as she explained the company to him. "Matthew, they gave me all the information on this company, beginning with the two brothers who immigrated from Ireland. This family had so many hardships: diseases that killed most of their families, the wars, and, of course, the weather. I mean, they have seen it all. It makes me proud to be part of this family. That doesn't mean I want to take it over or even live here. But I do want to see it stay strong. And look here." She slid Colin's five-year plan for expansion in front of Matthew.

"What am I looking at?"

"I asked Colin to see areas they could grow in, and his number one idea was to expand to other areas on the East Coast."

"Okay," he said, trying to appease her. But when he looked harder, he noticed a paper Agnes had added, suggesting

Savannah as a possible site. "What is this?" he asked, pointing to her addition.

"This is just an idea I wanted to discuss with you."

Matthew nodded while trying to hide the excitement he felt.

"When we went in the boat that day, you explained the bay on the side of my property and the deeper creek in the back. You said the oysters tasted perfect, but they had been picked over by all the terrapin from Barbee's Pavilion."

"That's right. They were wiped out, so there were none left to spawn."

"Well, the oysters here definitely do spawn. Wexford even has a hatchery. These reports say they produce millions of seeds each year. Sometimes, they even release them to the wild, under bridges or places where they're trying to build up the reefs. One of Colin's growth areas is to sell their seedlings. What if we buy seedlings from Prince Edward Island to replenish what the terrapin ate?"

Matthew pulled all the paperwork around him but only half-read the information. He didn't need to think about it. "This is a hell of an idea, Agnes."

"I know, right? But you would have to be my partner. You know everything about oysters, and I only need them for my stew." She stopped talking, then locked eyes with him. "I need to get home, Matthew. Can you make that happen for us while I finish writing all this up?"

He said only one word, "Yes," then leaned over to seal the deal with a kiss.

As he walked out of the mess hall, he stopped at the window one last time. She was already deep into her plans, writing like a fiend. She had saved him when he moved back to Savannah and showed him how to be in a loving relationship. Now, she had saved him with the possibility of his dream job, working with oysters in Savannah. He would never forget this moment—the second he knew he wanted to spend the rest of his life with Agnes Reed.

Agnes watched Prince Edward Island growing smaller in the distance. As the plane climbed, she could just make out the Blockhouse Point Lighthouse and how the red clay beach separated the snow from the ocean. "Goodbye, Prince Edward Island," she whispered.

Matthew rubbed the side of her arm. "Are you okay?" he asked.

Her heart swirled as she looked into his gray eyes. "Yes, I'm actually better than okay, and I now know why I was supposed to come: for closure. They should all just be getting up. They're going to be shocked to find us gone. Still, they'll find the letters in the kitchen and hopefully have a plan for the future."

He leaned over and kissed her softly, lingering an extra second or two on her lips. Pulling away, he whispered, "I think you're incredible, Agnes. What you've given everyone is an answered prayer. I know it is for me."

She smiled in response. "And you're an answered prayer for me." She gave in to a second kiss, long and full of meaning. She pulled away slowly, taking in each feature of Matthew's handsome face. How could she be so lucky? She had loved him for so long. Her inner self, the one who had been burned by him in the past, began to surface. *I'm not good enough for him; he's going to leave me again,* said the voice in her head.

Matthew laced his fingers through hers. Clearing his throat, he said, "I need to talk about something with you."

He's about to break up with me. I knew it was too good to be true, she thought as she whispered, "Okay."

"I don't know how it's done anymore. It used to be a courtship, but now our society has gotten scared to commit."

He turned in the airplane seat to look her in the eyes before announcing, "I don't want to date anyone else. And I certainly don't want you to date anyone else. You're my one and only. I know it sounds old-fashioned, but can I," he cleared his throat, "court you?"

Her stomach did somersaults as a smile spread across her face. Had he somehow heard her doubts? She replayed what he had just said with the steadiest voice she could muster. "You're my one and only, too. Yes!"

45

GOODBYE LETTERS

Gladys' slippers shuffled across the kitchen's cold wood floors. She shivered as the chill crept up her bare legs and pulled her robe tightly across her chest. The smell of coffee wafted through the air, making Gladys grin eagerly. In all her years of living at the oyster house, no one had ever put on the coffee for her. It was nice to have someone else in the house who enjoyed coffee as much as she did. No, it was more than that. It was nice to have Agnes so near to her.

She made her usual oatmeal, poured herself a cup of coffee, and walked towards the table. It wasn't until she set her breakfast down that she noticed the two letters propped against the lazy Susan, one with Colin's name and one with hers. Beside the letters sat the stack of records that Agnes had been given the day before, with several handwritten sheets of paper clipped to the front. Gladys picked up her letter and began to read.

Dear Gladys,
    Thank you for bringing me to Cavendish and being so

open in our conversation yesterday morning. It's fulfilling for a person to know their roots, and you gave me mine. I realize your life has not been an easy one, and I can't imagine the sorrow of losing not only a son but virtually your whole family. Know that I'm grateful for the decisions that you made for me. I look forward to our many conversations and meetings in the future.

Your granddaughter,
Agnes

Gladys flipped through the papers Agnes had prepared for the company, set them back in place, and then reread her personal letter. She was so deep in thought that she didn't hear Colin enter the kitchen.

"I sure do love the smell of coffee. Thank you for putting it on for us," Colin commented.

"Not me. Agnes," she answered.

"Ah, our chef, who just happens to own our company," he replied.

Gladys whipped her head in his direction. The annoyance in her eyes scared him, so he held up his hands in surrender, saying, "Whoa, I was just joking. I'm excited about our new business plan."

"They're gone," Gladys blurted out.

"Who's gone?"

"Agnes and Matthew. They must have left early this morning."

Colin plopped down into one of the kitchen chairs. "Why? Why would she leave? We were supposed to sit down together and devise a plan today. How could she just abandon us?"

"I think you need to read this," she answered.

He acknowledged her with a nod and picked up the handwritten letter on top of the files. He began reading out loud.

Dear Gladys and Colin,

    I finished the business plan for Wexford Oyster Company last night. I'm excited by the many possibilities for the company and for each of us. I'll never forget my time in Cavendish with both of you.

    Love, Agnes

Colin glanced up at Gladys with confusion. "Flip to the last sheet," she added.

He shuffled through the papers until he reached the last page, where Agnes relinquished control of the Oyster Company. "Well, I'll be!" he remarked.

"You'll be the owner of this business is what you'll be," she snipped. Closing her eyes, she took a deep breath. When she opened them, she reached over to Colin and patted his hand. Calmly, she said, "Now, let's review this business plan together."

He pulled his chair closer to Gladys, and they slowly began to go through the many pages, one by one. When they got to the end, they read through it again, this time stopping after reading the last page.

"She certainly left no stone unturned," Colin remarked. "But all the changes she suggests are based on us buying you out. She's reviewed the partnership agreement. If we follow the financing option, Wexford Oyster Company would be independently owned in seven years, and you would have the proceeds you need for you and Patrick. Plus, if we could put some of my ideas in place, it would cut the time significantly."

Gladys nodded her head in agreement, repeating his words in her head. *Seven years. I don't have seven years. And Patrick surely doesn't have seven years, either.* She turned to Colin and said, "Maybe there's another way. I'll look back through this again and try to come up with more options." She knew there was only one option for her, and it was based on something no one else in the world knew.

∼

Colin jogged along the path. Although the temperature was still below freezing, the snow had melted along the gravel. He thought about Agnes and everything she had done for him. How could he ever pay her back?

As he passed the cemetery, he remembered his conversation with Agnes. No one had ever explained adoption to him the way that Agnes had. *Why have I always felt like an outsider, like I'm not fully part of the family?* He wondered, surprised when his mind flashed to Gladys' face. He then thought about how Gladys' face lit up when she talked to Agnes. "I'll never be good enough for her," he uttered, and the reality of his statement hurt his heart.

He continued down the path, thinking back to childhood memories. He didn't remember his natural father and only vaguely remembered Henri and Maria. Papa Pat had raised him. It had always been just the two of them. He had no memories of Gladys on a day-to-day basis and felt like she was only around on holidays and long weekends. But how could that be? Surely, he was mistaken.

His run slowed to a walk as the path opened to the cliffs overlooking the ocean. He found his favorite spot on the large red boulder overlooking the water as he continued to search his mind for special moments with Gladys. He could picture himself learning to drive, graduating from high school, getting his various boater's licenses, and being out on the water. His papa was in every memory.

The truth of the matter hit him square in the face harder than the Northeastern wind blowing off the water; he was raised without a mother present. He had felt sorry for Agnes when she arrived. "They had sent her off to be adopted while they kept me," he had thought. And although his thoughts brought him guilt, a small part of it flattered him. But the truth is that Agnes was raised by a very active mother and father, and they loved her deeply.

Another gust of wind hit him hard; he shoved his hands deep into his pocket for protection. That's when he found Agnes' letter. He had been wearing his jacket the morning Agnes had left but had been so preoccupied with taking over the company that he had never read it. But there it was, still in the pocket where he had put it. Pulling it out, he noticed his name written in cursive on the front. He opened it and began to read.

> Dear Colin,
>
> I must tell you that this trip to Cavendish has been different than I ever expected. I never came looking for my birth family, but Gladys came looking for me. I wasn't sure why, but I do now that I've been to Cavendish. She wants to settle the company. I'm very sorry that I didn't know Patrick earlier, but Gladys told me I am a constant reminder of the loss of her son. That pain is too much for her to bear.
>
> The best thing that happened to me in Cavendish was getting to know you. I can't believe I've had family in Cavendish my whole life, and I didn't even know it. I look forward to getting to know you better.
>
> In looking over the company, especially over the past ten years, your name is repeatedly mentioned. I know how much it means to you, and it makes me happy to know that your dream of owning it will one day come true. I ask only one thing. Please consider Savannah as one of your East Coast subsidiaries. And I know just the place in the Low Country where you can start a new farm. Come see me, and I'll show you.
>
> With love, Agnes
>
> P.S.—I let you win our race down the cemetery trail. I'd love a re-match.

46

THE SPIRIT WORLD

Agnes had never been so happy to get home. When Matthew brought her luggage inside, he wanted to stay a while. But she had asked him to come back for dinner, pretending to have things to catch up on. Secretly, she wanted to check on the café, but more than that, she wanted to spend time with the horses.

The idea still made her laugh. She was worried about horses that obviously required zero attention anymore. Only, in her mind, they still did. Just like any other neglected animal, these horses craved her attention. No, it was more than that; they craved her acknowledgment.

When Matthew's truck pulled out of the driveway, she went looking for them. She walked outside, but the yard was quiet. She continued to walk further back on the property towards the shed, but still, there was nothing. She thought about the direction they always seemed to come from, so she walked to the edge of the woods that separated the shed from the bay. Standing still, she closed her eyes and let her mind relax.

She heard the horses deep in the woods before she felt

them. The sound of galloping approached quickly, encircling her in a whirlwind. Within seconds, she felt the wet of a snout lifting her hand. Then, a gentle nudge on her back. She smiled as she opened her eyes to nothingness. "I've missed you guys, but now I'm home for good," she told them. And somehow, for the first time ever, she could almost make out their shapes. Almost. She moved from one to the other, trying to count how many. "Are there nine of you?" she asked the roaming spirits, wondering, not for the first time, why they were on her property. She had always been told that animals didn't have souls, a rule she could never fully grasp. But if they didn't have souls, how would they have spirits? But that wasn't really the problem at hand. The most baffling issue was how she was able to communicate with them.

After saying her goodbyes, she walked back to the house.

Pulling her suitcase down the hallway, she was surprised when she saw the kitchen light pop on. "Oh no, not you, too," she said aloud and was rewarded by the sound of one of the kitchen cabinets opening. Leaving her luggage sitting in the hallway, she walked into the kitchen. In the middle of the table was the box. The same box that had been left for her the day she moved into the house.

"How did you wind up in my kitchen again?" she asked the box. However, she knew the answer: Lottie.

Just like before, she shuffled through the various items inside, each one now making sense. The shed key, the deeds to the house and restaurant, and the address in Cavendish. It wasn't until she came to the envelope with pictures that she paused. "I didn't know any of the people in these photos; I'll just put them back inside the envelope," she mumbled.

"Look again." The voice had come from behind.

Agnes jumped from her seat, spinning around so fast that the chair fell over, but no one was there. She looked down at her shaking hands and took a deep breath to steady her nerves. When she was finally in control of her emotions, she repeated the words she had just heard. "Look again?" she asked the open space, then responded, "Okay."

Picking the chair up from the floor, she sat down quickly and began examining each black and white photo. She could make out Lottie and her grandmother, Elizabeth, but all the other faces and locations were mysterious. Then she spotted Gladys. Once she recognized her, she realized Gladys was in almost every photo. She was always just outside the group. There was a photo of the whole family; the three girls were in school uniforms. All faces were in full smiles, but Gladys wore a smirk. Agnes recognized that smirk; she had seen it more than once. Then, there was a picture of the three sisters standing on the pier. Lottie and Elizabeth had their arms draped around one another, but Gladys stood a foot away with her hands on her hips. Her head was tilted, and her eyes cut straight to the person holding the camera. There was a random photo of Lottie with someone she didn't recognize. Turning it over, it read, "Lottie and Annie". She had no memories of anyone named Annie, so she flipped to the last photo. It was of a very young Lottie and Benjamin. Lottie was showing off her hand. Was it an engagement photo? "Ah. Look at y'all," Agnes said. "You are so cute."

Again, the voice came. "Look harder."

This time, Agnes didn't jump. She only did what she was told. Holding the picture closer, she noticed Gladys in the background. She was licking ice cream from a cone while she watched the couple. The look on her face sent chills down Agnes' spine. It wasn't jealousy or disgust; it was the look of someone who held a secret and was amused by it.

"Oh wow," Agnes said out loud. "What does this mean?" She flipped the photo over to see a date on the back. *When did she go missing? Hmm. I can't remember,* she said to herself. *There's something else. What is it?* She wasn't sure why, but she pictured Bonaventure Cemetery.

I'll run by the café and then out to the cemetery before dark, she told herself. Something made her turn back to the photos, so she tucked the box under her arm and ran out the door.

The sign reading "Aggie's" was the first thing she noticed when she pulled up to the restaurant. The second thing she saw was the tribe trying to hang it. "What are y'all doing here?" she asked.

"We heard you were back in town and wanted you to be excited when you came by the restaurant," Stephanie explained.

"How did you know I was back?" she asked, but she knew how fast word traveled around Savannah. "Never mind. I'm just glad you're here. I've missed you." She hugged each of their necks before pulling out her keys and entering the restaurant.

They followed in behind, pelting her with questions about her trip. "How was your trip?" was the first question. Agnes briefly explained Prince Edward Island and her travels before they asked the second question. "How is Matthew?" The smile on her face gave her away, and the tribe began to tease her. They continued to talk about Matthew: his looks, how nice he was, and finally, whether he was a good kisser.

As soon as everyone was inside, her friends began raiding the pantry.

"How do you not have anything to eat here?" Maggie answered.

"I haven't been here," Agnes replied. "There might be something in that back corner." Her friends searched like savages but grunted when all they found were crackers.

"Let's run and grab dinner at Johnny Harris," Jan suggested.

Agnes answered first. "I'd love that, but I have a quick errand to run. I can meet you there."

"Let's go with Agnes on her errand and leave our cars here," Kathleen suggested. When they all agreed, she added, "I call shotgun!"

47

THORNS

One by one, they piled into the car. Kathleen fiddled with the radio as they traveled down Victory Drive and turned onto Skidaway Road. But when Agnes took another turn onto Bonaventure, the mood in the car changed. "Where are we going?" they asked.

"I just need to see something real fast. It will only take a second," she answered.

"Where will you be seeing this something?" Latrice asked again.

"Uh. Bonaventure Cemetery," Agnes answered.

"Oh, hell no. You know I don't do ghosts," Stephanie bellowed from the middle of the back seat.

"Every person who dies doesn't turn into a ghost," Jan added.

Stephanie continued to shake her head. "No, but I don't want to meet *anyone who* has."

"Well, you don't really have a choice, do you? You're shoved in between three people in the backseat," Maggie remarked.

Stephanie bellowed, "Well, I'm not leaving the car."

Kathleen rolled down her window as the car traveled down

Bonaventure's twists and turns. "I don't feel so well," she announced.

"It's usually me that gets car sick," Agnes responded. "Do you want me to pull over?"

Kathleen leaned her head out the window. "No. I don't think it's the driving. There's a weird smell in the car that's making me nauseous."

Every nose in the car began to sniff except for Jan.

"Oh my gosh, I smell it, too," Latrice added.

"It smells like cheese," Maggie remarked.

Jan finally broke. "I was hungry. I grabbed a few squares of cheese from Agnes' refrigerator, but the first piece was so nasty that I couldn't eat the rest, so I shoved it in my purse."

"That cheese has been in there for so long. It's probably moldy," Agnes answered.

Jan opened her purse, and the smell filled the car. "Ugh, I don't feel well either," she announced.

"Give me your damn purse, Jan," Latrice bellowed. Freeing the cheese from a folded paper towel, she tossed it out the window. Kathleen continued taking in large gulps of air as the smell of moldy cheese escaped out the window.

Agnes turned off the radio out of respect as the car bumped through the Bonaventure Cemetery gate. She had spent so much time at the cemetery with Lottie that it felt like coming home. Looking down the azalea-lined dirt roads, Agnes commented, "What a beautiful place to be laid to rest."

Latrice agreed, "It sure is, except . . ." She let the word hang in the air until everyone was eager to hear the ending. "Except for the ones that are not resting."

"I hate y'all," Stephanie said under her breath while reaching out to hold Kathleen's hand. The whole car burst out laughing and continued to tease her. When Agnes stopped the car in the middle of one of the lanes, she was the first one to hop out. Each of them followed, climbing out in the order they got in—all except for Stephanie, who sat frozen in the backseat. Walking around the car, they found Agnes balancing on the coping around their family plot.

"I should be ashamed of myself for letting this go," Agnes mumbled.

"It looks fine to me," Latrice announced as she blew past Agnes and walked towards Lottie's grave. Stopping suddenly, she cried out, "Ow!" and hopped over to sit on the large tree trunk. "Look at this," she said to her friends. "Help me."

Latrice began pulling sand spurs from her feet. She tried removing them with her fingernails, but some still stuck into her fingers.

"Who wears open-toe shoes in January?" Maggie asked.

"I just got my toenails done, and I had a big luncheon with the City Commissioners today. Don't judge!" Glancing up at Maggie, she added, "When was the last time you wore anything other than those orthopedic-looking shoes anyway?"

"My shoes are practical and comfortable," Maggie snipped.

"Well, that certainly sounds sexy," Kathleen added.

Maggie whipped her head towards Kathleen and pointed down at her shoes. "You call those sexy?"

"My feet are swollen from being pregnant. You just wait," Kathleen answered.

"I definitely can wait if I have to wear geriatric shoes like those," Jan teased.

Stephanie's voice cried out from the car. "Hey! Hey, what are y'all looking at?"

"Don't turn around. Act like you don't hear her," Agnes mumbled.

The group gathered around Latrice, each trying to help her pull spurs from her feet and fingers.

"Hey. Don't y'all hear me?" Stephanie yelled.

Jan turned toward the car and got reprimanded by the group. "Don't look, Jan. She's so nosy she'll eventually come to us." Talking among themselves, they continued to help Latrice while keeping a side-eye towards Stephanie. They giggled when they watched her exit the car and run in their direction.

"Hey. What's going on?" she asked. Looking down at the group, she added, "Are those thorns? Oh no. It's not a good sign if you get into thorns in the cemetery. That's how the dead get back at you."

Latrice gave her a look. It was Latrice's specialty. She could freeze water with those eyes. "Well, I guess someone's trying to get you back then because you're covered in them, too."

Stephanie looked down on her pants to find the hem covered in thorns. Terror spread across her face, and she began to run back towards the car.

Agnes quickly clicked the automatic lock. "I don't want stickers in my car," she yelled out.

"I'll go after her," Kathleen announced.

Agnes added, "And I'll go get what I came for." She walked towards the tombstones. Benjamin and Lottie shared a double marker with their last name across the top. Underneath, it read, "Joined in Holy Matrimony with the date of November 12, 1938. She first looked at Lottie's name. She paused and said a prayer, then moved to Benjamin's. She had never noticed before, but his full name was Henri Benjamin. Her mind quickly jumped to another tombstone; this one was in Cavendish. Although the last name was different, the rest was the same. Henri Benjamin, her birth father, who was born on February 6, 1939.

"Coincidence?" she whispered, knowing the answer before she heard it. There's no such thing as coincidences. She wandered over to Gladys' tombstone. A chill ran up her spine. *It's so odd to look down on a grave knowing the person is still alive,* she thought. Her eyes were drawn back to the date. All doubts were gone in that instant. Gladys had been pregnant when she left Savannah.

48

MANLY

Agnes woke to the smell of coffee. Stumbling into the kitchen, she found a note sitting in front of the pot.

I was too excited to sleep, so I got an early start. Grab a cup of coffee and walk out on the porch to say, "Hello."

She did as she was told, pouring herself a cup of coffee while thinking how happy it made her that Matthew knew where she hid the stow-away key. Then she threw on a pair of jeans and a Notre Dame sweatshirt that was worn soft from the wear. Stepping onto the porch, she first noticed Matthew's sailboat moored once again in the creek out front. She smiled, happy that he would be nearby. The sound of hammering drew her attention, but the openness of the marsh made it hard to pinpoint which direction it was coming from. She began to scan the marsh and was shocked to see Matthew out in the bay.

She walked down the back steps toward the shoreline and stopped beside his small Jon boat. Matthew was in the middle of the bay, swinging a hammer. Each time it made contact with the oyster rake, she cringed. The sound of shell breaking against the steel of the hammer was deafening. Nevertheless, she couldn't pull her eyes away from Matthew in his form-fitting waders. *Am I ogling?* she asked herself, but then she reasoned that there was something about a man doing manly things that makes a woman stop and appreciate the sight.

Something drew his attention, and when he looked up, he noticed her standing on the shore. She had just taken a large gulp of coffee that she suddenly couldn't swallow. His smile was from ear to ear on his unshaven face. Either he was happy from being on the water or seeing her. She hoped it was the latter. He raised his hand to acknowledge her, and her heart began to race. *Oh my gosh, I love this man*, she thought as the coffee started to choke her. She coughed and sputtered until she spit it out. Looking back at him, she noticed the concern in his eyes, so she gave him a thumbs-up. Her face burned with embarrassment. *Could you be any more awkward?* she asked herself, backing away from the bay. However, when she glanced back at him one last time, she realized he was still watching her. She waved and pointed up toward the house. This time, he acknowledged her with a thumbs-up.

She shivered as she walked back into the house, so she grabbed the soft cotton throw from the couch's arm and pulled it around her shoulders. Although Savannah's winters were nothing like the cold she felt on Prince Edward Island, forty-degree breezes through the marsh still sent a chill up her spine.

Snuggling into a spot at the end of the couch, she tucked her legs underneath her and gazed out the window. She could barely make out Matthew's shape in the marsh, but she could definitely hear him. The rhythmic sound of the hammer continued to ring through the air, but this time, it didn't bother her. She loved knowing he was nearby.

Today would be another busy day at the café. She would be opening her doors the following week, and there was much to be done. At least she wouldn't be at the restaurant alone. The Oyster Stew Crew would be working the whole day, too. Colin had come through on their agreement and had delivered enough oysters for her company to complete all of their backorders of stew. Colin also gave her the family discount as agreed upon.

She could hardly wait to hear Gary's opinion on the new oysters. Although the grand opening of Aggie's was a little bit later than she had initially planned, the customers would be delighted to see the return of "Lottie's Old-Fashioned Oyster Stew" on the menu.

Agnes began saying her morning prayers as she drove to work. Immediately, she started belting out her intentions, "God, please help me with...," but she stopped. A nun at Notre Dame had shared the PAL method she used every time she prayed. She explained to Agnes that the P was for praise. So, Agnes silently praised. She then moved to the A, which was for asking. She silently asked for help, which took up a good bit of her car ride. As she turned onto Waters Ave, she moved into the last letter of L, which stands for listen. This was always the most challenging part for Agnes, so she wasn't upset that she only had a few minutes of her car ride left.

Pulling into the parking lot, she noticed her mom sitting in her car. Agnes had only been to their house a couple of times since she had returned from Prince Edward Island, so her mom had started coming to Aggie's. She told Agnes that she had extra time and wanted to help out, but Agnes knew there was more. Her mom had been worried about her ever since Gladys had come into the picture. Agnes hated worrying her more, but she needed her mom's advice.

As they filled the salt and pepper shakers, Agnes asked, "Mom, did you find anything odd about Gladys?"

Her mom stopped pouring the salt, leaving the shaker half-filled. Agnes knew her mom like the back of her hand; she rarely paused before offering her opinion. However, she was usually spot-on. "Agnes, I've tormented myself over your relationship with Gladys. Your father told me it was just jealousy, but it was so much more than that. There is a coldness about her that I don't understand. My mom and Lottie were nothing like her. You could look in their eyes and feel the warmth, but Gladys always looks like she's plotting something. I don't understand it."

"Can I share something with you, Mom?"

Her mother set the saltshaker on the table and gave Agnes her full attention. Agnes explained Gladys' breakdown, looking over the marsh, and retold her story. Then, she shared the newspaper headlines. Last, she shared how she and Matthew thought she acted odd the whole time in Canada.

Her mom nodded, listening intently. Then Agnes remembered the tombstones. "Did you know my birthfather had the same name as Lottie's husband?"

Her mom leaned in closer. "What?"

"I visited my father's grave in Cavendish. His name was Henri Benjamin. Henri with an I. That's quite a coincidence, isn't it?"

Her mom's hand flew to her face. "Oh my gosh. You don't think..."

"Mom, I kind of do. But how can we be sure?"

Her mother thought for a moment, then answered. "We

need to get the date that Gladys went missing. I believe it's on her fake tombstone in Bonaventure. Then, we need to get your father's day of birth."

Agnes took her mom's hand. "Great minds think alike. I did that, Mom. Gladys went missing in July 1938. Lottie and Benjamin were married that November and my father was born on February 6, 1939."

"Oh my gosh. Benjamin was your grandfather. I wonder if he knew?" She quietly added, "I wonder if Lottie knew?"

Agnes thought about all the clues that had been laid before her and all the times she had heard Lottie's whispers. Squeezing her mom's hand, she quietly said, "Oh yeah, she knows, Mom. She definitely knows."

"I'm not going to ask why you are speaking of Lottie in the present tense," her mom added.

Agnes walked around the table and kissed her mom on the forehead, "She's only in the next room," she said without thinking.

"I've heard that somewhere before," her mom answered.

With a knowing smile, Agnes added, "And you'll probably be hearing it several more times in the future."

Confusion spread across her mom's face as she processed what Agnes said. Finally, she only nodded with acknowledgment. "I love you, my girl," she said, adding, "Now get back to work."

49

FILTERING WATER

Since their return from Prince Edward Island the month before, Matthew had stayed busy getting the area around Mystic Lane ready. He first found Louey, who had taught him everything he knew about oystering. Matthew was excited when Louey agreed to ride out to the site and give his opinion on the oysters in the bay. When he arrived, he stood on the bank for the longest time, breathing in the smell of the marsh. "You know, it's not like this in Shellman's Bluff. I had family there, so when the oysters ran dry in Isle of Hope, I moved right down and set up my oyster business there. But this area is a sweet spot."

He expertly went to different areas in the bay, chiseling away several oysters to sample. "It's nice to see the oysters repopulating this area. They had been picked over for years. But not by me. The old terrapin turtles left over from Barbee's Pavilion ate them up." Matthew nodded in acknowledgment. "You see, the adult females had the most powerful jaws. They would eat all the oysters in this area. But they must have moved on when the food was gone. You gotta watch for them coming back."

Matthew explained how his oysters would be enclosed in baskets and laughed when he saw Louey's confusion. Louey's only reply was, "I don't know about that." After another second or two, Louey began to smile. His big, toothless grin lit up his eyes. He patted Matthew on his shoulder and added, "Now this, I gotta see."

Matthew's next call was to the Ossabaw Island Institute of Oceanography. They were intrigued enough to ride out to the site. After discussing his ideas, they helped Matthew develop an additional plan.

They explained, "Oysters are the best water filtration systems around. Harbors like New York have been renewed by bringing in new oyster habitats along the Hudson River. Your company, which operates out of Isle of Hope, helps our waterways, but imagine what could happen if a filtration rake were set up in the Savannah River. The State of Georgia could provide you with the space."

Matthew shook his head, wondering how he had come full circle back to the one thing that he loved. When he answered, he spoke from the heart. "I don't even know if this first oyster farm is a definite, but I really hope everything goes as planned. Finding ways to clean our waterways is something I feel strongly about, and I would love to speak with you further about these possibilities."

As soon as they parted, Matthew walked around the bay area. He had been working hard, and it was finally taking shape. *Colin should be able to gauge the area at this point*, he thought. He knew it was time when he hiked to the other side of the property where the deep water ran. Both Louey and the Ossabaw Institute of Oceanography had been able to envision his plans and had been excited about them. He hoped that Colin would see things the same way.

∽

Matthew wandered around the shoreline. Would there be a way to put a dock or a walkway of some kind to connect the bay and the deeper water in the back? The land was deep with undergrowth and trees and sat as high as Bluff Road. He began walking slowly along the edge to see if there were any obstacles he needed to be aware of. He cursed when his toe hit a piece of concrete and was happy no one was around to hear him cursing out loud. Pulling the pine straw and dirt that had settled for years from around its border, Matthew could just make out some writing, but it was so old he couldn't read it.

"Is this a grave marker?" he muttered and began looking for more. Surprisingly, he found two more just like this one. They were all in a row and were still intact, although the writing had been badly worn. Once again, he began to curse. Gravesites had been known to stop projects. He had just read in the paper how the Atlanta airport had to stop its expansion because the airstrips had run over a cemetery. Maybe these were family plots. He would remember to ask Agnes.

As he walked around, he found more markers. They were just small concrete squares as if the person wanted to acknowledge a death but didn't need or have money for a tombstone.

As he continued walking, he thought about his conversations that day. He almost felt ungrateful for talking about projects other than the one at hand. Agnes was trusting him to get an oyster farm up and running on the water around her property; why would he be looking for his next gig? Although he didn't go looking, it came looking for him. He was still deep in thought when he reached her house.

She must have seen him coming because she called out, "Hello, my handsome oysterer."

He smiled at her as he walked up the stairs, slipped off his boots, and entered the back sitting room.

"It's cold out there. You want a cup of coffee?"

"Maybe a cold beer instead," Matthew remarked as they moved into the kitchen.

"How did your meetings go today?" she asked.

Agnes had been so busy getting ready to open the café but still remembered his meetings. Her one question eased his mind, and he happily shared his conversation with Ossabaw Island Institute of Oceanography.

Agnes yelped with delight. "Oh my gosh, Matthew, that's wonderful news. And you are just the man to do it. You'll already know about oyster farming and love Savannah's waterways. That would be a dream come true."

As she jumped into his arms, he hugged her tightly, wondering why he ever doubted she would be anything less than supportive. She only wanted what was best for him—nothing more and nothing less.

"You think you could love a man who wore waders year after year?" he asked.

"I think I could handle that. If you answer me just one question."

"Anything," he replied.

She pulled on the strap of his grey Orvis fishing bib that resembled overalls. "What do you wear underneath those waders?" she whispered as she pulled one strap down from his shoulder.

"You really want to know?" he whispered as he nibbled on her ear lobe. She nodded, so he pulled the other shoulder off and let the waders fall to the ground.

Agnes burst out laughing, then backed up to get a better look. "Red and white polka-dot long johns? Are those standard issue?" she teased.

He pulled her back in close as his voice became serious. "Agnes, I'm not a man who will ever be clean-cut. I'll always have mud under my fingernails and long johns under my waders. But I promise you, if you'll have me, I want to be with you. I'll always put you first in life, but most of all, I'll always love you."

Startled by his seriousness, she looked into his eyes, searching his face for sincerity.

"What? Too much?" he asked with a shrug.

She wrapped her arms around his neck. "No. The perfect amount. And there is nothing in this world I would rather have than you."

50

AU REVOIR

Gladys parked along the street and began to gather her belongings. Glancing at the small box made her stomach lurch. "Can I do this?" she uttered, letting her hand hover above it, then scooped up the box and set it in her purse.

She had always loved Montreal. Its beauty, its history, and, most of all, its size. *Could they find me here?* She wondered. Still, she knew she must go farther and put at least one ocean between her and North America. She had found a few islands off the coast of Greece where she was interested. Somewhere warmer where she could finally relax. The world said she'd been dead for fifty years, and in some ways, she had felt as if she were. Leaving Savannah hadn't been as bad as she thought. She had wanted to get away anyway, but being forced to leave by thugs had never sat well with her. Benjamin would have protected her if she had only known she was pregnant before she left. Instead, she was forced to marry someone she could never love and claimed to get pregnant on her wedding night. Poor Patrick. He had been so easy to convince.

She shook her head at the memory, knowing that thoughts

of being pregnant would only lead to the hole in her heart left by Henri's death. She had done everything she could to push his memory from her mind; it just hurt so much. She had honestly believed she could forget as soon as she got rid of all the reminders. She had been so naïve. And with that, she was left with her only regret: Agnes. How in the world had she let her go? And how would she live the rest of her life without her?

As she turned onto Rue St. Paul, the cold wind running through the funnel of buildings hit her in the face. Her eyes began to water, or were they already watering from the thought of losing Agnes again? She balanced on the cobblestone road, which was blocked off to traffic. It really was beautiful in Old Montreal. It reminded her so much of Paris. *Ah, Paris. I could settle there. I'll need to see how much money I make this time before I choose*, she reasoned.

Seeing the red sign hanging in the block ahead, she paused. La Galerie sur St. Paul had been good to her over the years, and everything she had sold to them had been high value and unmarked. She had even developed a relationship with the owner, Jean Claude, who always took her to lunch after their transactions. Her stomach growled thinking about the ossobuco at Marcella's. Would she have time for that today? *No! You have to stay focused. Tell your story, get your retirement money, and get the hell out,* she repeatedly told herself until she swung open the gallery door.

Gladys first sold the remaining diamonds, one by one. When Jean Claude stood and asked her to lunch, she pulled the small black box from her purse. The jeweler had his loupe over the piece in seconds, turning it from side to side under the magnifier while half-listening to Gladys' tale of the family heirloom she no longer desired.

Gladys made herself not look over her shoulder as she walked out the front door of La Galerie sur St. Paul. A slight twinge of guilt hit her hard. She knew the jeweled-covered brooch would fetch a pretty penny, but an expert buyer would recognize it. And if that happened, her long-term friend would lose everything. The guilt needled at her one last time. "Au Revoir," she whispered into the wind and vowed never to think of Jean Claude again.

Colin walked into the large kitchen. He could barely remember a time when it was full of people. He wondered if they could take in borders like they once did. Several men had asked, but Gladys had told him no every time. But Gladys wouldn't be there much longer; she would be moving to Charlottetown with Patrick. It saddened him to see how much Papa Pat had declined in the last few months. Still, there were good days every now and again. Like this morning when he visited, Patrick was about to play checkers with him. He thought back to when his papa had taught him how to play and what a sore loser he had been when Papa Pat won. *That seems like a lifetime ago.*

Gladys was gone once again. Although it had been a quiet week, Colin had stayed busy working on different ideas for the business. He even planned a trip to Savannah the following week to discuss adding an oyster site. He turned up his third cup of coffee, rinsed the mug, and set it on the green rubber drying rack when he heard the knock on the door.

"Coming," he called out as the knock came again, then opened the door to a man holding a briefcase. Colin looked at his suit and clean-cut hair and knew instantly he wasn't from Cavendish. "Can I help you with something?"

"Are you Colin O'Hara?"

"Yes, sir, that's me."

"I have some papers for you to sign."

After ushering the man to the kitchen table, he pulled out a stack of papers.

"This is a paper turning over the shares for Wexford Oyster Company from Mr. Patrick O'Hara to Mr. Colin O'Hara."

"Wait, please explain."

"Your mother holds power of attorney for your father, who can no longer make decisions. She turned over all the remaining company shares to you before she left."

"Left?"

The man raised his eyebrows. "Yes, she's moved out of the country. The company's assets include three houses along the bluff, the production company, dock house, nine boats, and all land and equipment within these boundaries." Pointing to a map, the man made a swoop all the way to the red cliffs.

"It's all mine?"

"Yes. And one more thing. An account has been set up with payment deposited for Mr. Patrick O'Hara's care for twenty years. It's in your name, too. Congratulations. The finalized paperwork will be sent to you in two weeks. Good day," he snipped, closed his briefcase, and stood to leave.

Colin looked around the kitchen, noticing things for the first time. *I own everything,* he thought. *Right down to the coffee cup in my hand.* Taking one last sip, he realized how much better coffee tasted when you actually own the cup. He wasn't sure why she left, but he was grateful for the gift she had given him.

51

SOUTHERN CHARM

As Agnes sipped her coffee, she thought of her grand opening. Wondering how the ad she placed in the newspaper turned out, she quickly walked to the front yard and returned with the paper. Situating herself on the couch, she opened the paper to the headlines. "Items From the Legendary Jewel Heist off the Coast of Savannah Recovered." Interested, she continued reading, pulling out the tidbits of essential facts: The robbery occurred on July 2, 1938. The victim was billionaire William Sandry. There were three thieves. A world-famous family heirloom, a brooch, and many other jewels were stolen. The brooch had been sold in Montreal last week.

A cold chill crept up Agnes' back as the words began to form in her mind. "Yes. You're right to question this in your mind. Look deeper," came Lottie's voice. The whispers were always in Lottie's voice.

What does this mean? She wondered, trying to align the puzzle pieces. *Three thieves? Three. How many men were in Gladys' story?* She played it over in her mind. *Three men were executed on the back of the yacht. Could those be the same three men, or was it a coincidence? There's no such thing as coincidences,* she told herself.

"I need to let Gladys know. She could be in danger," Agnes mumbled.

The loud thud startled her. The hardback book from her coffee table hit the floor so hard that Agnes spilled her coffee. She looked around the room for the culprit but knew who it was. "Think," came the voice. "Montreal?"

The seed of doubt hit her hard. Once that seed was planted, she knew she must see it to the end. Turning to Lottie's favorite chair, she muttered, "I don't have all the pieces in place, but I promise I'll keep looking and talk with Colin when he gets here for his visit. But for now, I'm needed at Aggie's."

"I need to talk with you about Gladys," was the first thing Colin said when Agnes opened her door.

"Welcome to Savannah, Colin. It's great to see you again. Come on in," Agnes replied, motioning him into the house.

Colin nodded in acknowledgment. "Good ole' Southern charm. Everybody around here seems to have it, and I'll tell you what, I could get used to it," he said as he dropped his bags inside the doorway. He gave Agnes a double pat on the shoulder as he passed and began looking around her house.

"This is really nice," he said, moving from room to room. When he finally reached the back of the house, he walked straight out onto the porch. "Oh, wow!" he muttered as his eyes scanned the marsh. Agnes watched him as he breathed in heavily and exhaled with a smile. "There's oysters out there."

"Well, there better be," Matthew called out as he walked up from the bay. "You want to see them?"

That's all it took. Agnes lost him right then and there. The conversation he wanted to have about Gladys flew from his mind as soon as he smelled the salt water. *That's how it is with people who love to be near the ocean. When they smell salt water, all other thoughts disappear,* she thought. She followed them down to the bluff, listening to the two men talking. Matthew explained how he collected oysters in the bay as a boy and how they were the best-tasting oysters he had ever eaten.

"Oysters are always better when you pull them from the ocean yourself," Colin had interjected.

Agnes watched the two men; they had so much in common. They had lived very different lives but were now brought together over their love of the water.

She snuck away in the middle of their conversation. *They won't even know I'm gone.* But instead of returning to the house, she decided to drop into the shed. She hadn't been there in a couple of weeks. Between her grand opening, which had gone off perfectly, the thriving oyster stew business, and now the company with Matthew, she hadn't allowed herself time to relax. *I'm happy I took the whole day off to be with Colin,* she snickered, knowing she probably wouldn't see much of him.

Walking inside, she went straight to the big, comfy chair and plopped down. She loved Lottie's space in the shed and came out there often to relax. She wiggled herself into a comfortable spot and let her mind wander. Her eyes scanned the room blankly until they fell onto the open closet. *Why is the closet door open?* Then her eyes settled on the books—not just any books, the books with the blue ribbon.

"Go. Go get them," said the whisper in her head. Still, she listened. She pulled the stack from the closet, dusted them off, and brought them back to her comfy chair. Flipping on the small lamp on the side table, she carefully opened the top one and began reading. The first line took her breath away. *I met Agnes for the first time today.* She continued reading. *I didn't actually meet her, but I saw her. I pictured Gladys standing beneath a metal arched sign that read "Victoria Row," holding a screaming baby. I never knew where Gladys was; she never allowed me to know. But her guard was down at that moment, and she needed me.*

Agnes turned the pages quickly. Lottie had researched and found that Gladys was in Charlottetown.

Things aren't as they seem, although I'm not sure why. I found Gladys at her luxurious home in Charlottetown. How a small-town nurse married to an oysterer can afford such luxury is very confusing. I'm staying the night in the small cottage behind her house, #52 ½ to be exact. I'll be traveling back to Savannah tomorrow. My being here has made her extremely uncomfortable. One thing is for sure, she's not able to raise this sweet baby. I'm having Gladys bring her home to Ruthie.

"It was planned. Lottie knew she wanted Ruthie to raise me." Agnes sniffled. The tears quickly turned into a full cry. She read about Gladys coming to Savannah and hiding in Lottie's shed in case people were still looking for the lost jewels. Then she read about Gladys' betrayal.

I always had my suspicions, but I was naïve as a child. I knew Gladys always wanted more, but I didn't realize the lengths she would go to obtain it. She began acting differently towards me when Ben and I got engaged. I told myself that she didn't want me to leave the family. I know now that she was jealous of what I had. So, she tried to destroy it. Today, as Ruthie signed the adoption papers, I realized Gladys listed Agnes' birth parents' names. Agnes' father was named Henri Benjamin. It is no coincidence that my husband, the first Henri Benjamin, was Henri's father.

"Oh, Lottie. I'm so sorry," Agnes whispered as she turned the page.

I've told no one of my discoveries. Ben is so sick. The news would kill him. And although I'd like to strangle him myself for not telling me, I don't want the end of his life to be in turmoil.

Agnes stopped to wipe her eyes. She was so tired from crying. I need to get up. I need to go find Matthew and Colin, she thought. But once her eyes closed even for a brief moment, she was fast asleep. She felt a hand gently rubbing the top of her head and pictured Lottie smiling down at her. She struggled to open her eyes. The hand continued to stroke until she was able to open one eye to Matthew.

"You must have fallen asleep," he said quietly.

She smiled up at him, but her eyes moved to Colin. "Colin!" she yelled, bolting up. "Colin, I need to talk to you about Gladys."

Colin knelt beside her. "Yes. I know. She's gone."

"Gone?" she sputtered in confusion. "Gone where?"

"Well, I'm not sure, but I don't think she's ever returning. Although, I've come to realize that she was never really there anyway. Patrick was always my dad, but Gladys was just someone who floated in and out. We usually don't see the things we don't want to see. I know I didn't," Colin replied. "But you know what that old bird did? She relinquished the company to me. She gave me everything."

Agnes thought for a moment, "What about Patrick?"

"He's still at the house with me, and she set up a trust to care for him. I'm unsure where she came up with the money, but it's all been finalized."

Agnes reached down for Lottie's journal but stopped. She knew where Gladys got the money from, those stolen jewels. But Colin didn't need to know that. It was better for Colin to remember Gladys in a good light.

Agnes stood and gave Colin a hug. "I'm happy for you, Colin. You'll be great running Wexford Oyster Company."

Colin tilted his head as a soft smile moved across his face. "Thank you. And I can't wait until you guys are up and running, too."

52

TREASURE

Colin loved visiting Savannah. Agnes was able to share her life with him, showing him all there was to see her city. Still, in the end, his favorite experience was having Saturday lunch with her family. Colin was family, too. She was happy when Bobby, Chris, and Tim treated him as such. They teased and horsed around with him, then made him play basketball in the driveway.

After the game, Bobby pulled out camping chairs, and they sat around on the court talking. Tim pulled five beers out of the garage refrigerator and passed one to each of them. As they each popped open their cans, Colin turned to Agnes and asked, "Hey, when can I come back for another visit? I'd like to bring Tammy."

She slapped him on the arm. "Tammy? You're dating Tammy?" He began to look embarrassed, so she teased. "What's a fun and classy gal like my friend Tammy doing with a guy like you?" she kidded before adding, "I really like her. I'd love for you to bring her to Savannah."

Her brothers asked Colin questions about Canada, oysters,

and, of course, Tammy. Everyone enjoyed each other's company until it was time to leave.

Colin was very quiet on the ride home back to her house. When they approached Isle of Hope, he opened up. "You know, I've always felt sorry for you because you were pulled away from your home in Cavendish. I don't anymore. You are lucky; you grew up with a terrific family who loves you deeply."

Agnes nodded and turned to catch a quick glance at him before darting her eyes back to the tricky curves of La Roche Ave. "You're my family, too. I'm sorry it took me so long to find you, but I'm so happy I did." A stray tear slid down Agnes' cheek, and she quickly wiped it away.

"Ah, we'll have none of that," he said as he watched her take a turn in a direction he wasn't familiar with. "Where are we going?"

"There's somewhere I want you to see before you leave." She drove a bit further, then turned into the gates.

"Whoa," he whispered, which made Agnes smile. "What is this place?"

"You've seen most of Isle of Hope; I didn't want you to miss Wormsloe." She flashed her pass to the State Park ranger and parked her car near the gate. "This was the estate of Noble Jones, who arrived with General Oglethorpe from England. He was a fascinating man who served our colony well. There's a museum that tells all the history, but the most interesting thing for me is the land." She pointed down the oak-lined road, whose canopy almost shaded the road. "This is one of the most photographed places in Savannah."

"I can see why," he commented.

"It's also one and a half miles from one end to the other," she said as she leaned over, touched the ground, and stretched from side to side. "I usually drive to the end, then walk the trails on the property." She pulled her knees to her chest, one at a time. "But I have a better idea today."

He watched, and then recognition crept across his face. With a mischievous grin, he leaned back into a shin stretch, saying, "Do you really think you have it in you?"

"I've been running strong since the last time we raced, so yeah, I think I can take you." He nodded, so she announced, "The first person to reach the last tree is the champion of the world. 3 – 2 – 1 – Go!"

Colin had an early flight the following morning and wanted to walk the property with Agnes and Matthew before he left. "I really think you've got something here," he said as they walked towards the bay. Fog sat low over the water, hovering just enough to see its reflection in the water. "The fog is so strange here." he stated.

"Yes, it is. At first, I thought it was bad luck, like the man who is followed by a rain cloud. In contrast, it's like a blanket of protection for oysters, especially when the sun is beating down. Maybe that's why the land is named The Mystic," Agnes replied.

"Has it always been like this back here?" Colin asked.

"Oh, yeah. I swiped oysters from here as a boy. It's always been like this," Matthew chimed in.

Colin rubbed under his chin. "The Mystic. That's a pretty cool name. And The Mystic produces the most tasteful oysters. I tried a few myself from the bay. Oysters protected by Mother Nature."

"You're right. It's a pretty cool name." A smile broke out on Matthew's face as he turned to Agnes. "We've been wondering what to name our oysters. How about the obvious, Mystic Oysters?"

"Yes! Mystic Oysters from the lovely Isle of Hope, Georgia," she added, linking her elbows with Matthew and Colin's.

They silently watched the sun rise over the bay until a large Heron flew across the marsh. Colin broke the quiet, "I'll have oyster seeds ready whenever you want them, but I believe that's all I can do until I get established as the sole owner. Your water is perfect, but you must do a few things with the land, like clearing the woods for a dock and getting some equipment and a couple of larger boats."

"Give me a roundabout of how much you think we'll need?" Matthew asked.

"One hundred and fifty thousand. Maybe a little more. I know it's not ideal, but if you could give me a couple of years, I'd love to help with more than just the seeds." Colin added.

Matthew looked like someone had punched him in the gut as he locked eyes with Agnes.

"We'll figure this out," was all she said, but she felt the worry in her chest. *I guess that's what happens when you love someone: You worry for them constantly. But he doesn't have to worry alone.* What was that old adage? A problem shared is a problem halved? She nodded to herself and repeated it once more: "We'll figure this out together."

The added word captured his attention, and he offered a sexy smile. "Together, eh?"

When she nodded shyly, he was in front of her in half a second, picking her up until her feet left the ground. "Yes, we will, my dear. We'll figure this out together." Then, moving his lips to her ear, he added, "And it's sure gonna be fun figuring it out with you."

Colin cleared his throat, "All right, you two. Simmer down. Let's finish our walk before I need to leave. I met a deer on my walk yesterday on the backside of the property. I told him I'd check on him and say goodbye before I left."

Turning from the bay, they began to walk along the marsh line until they hit the woods. Matthew had made a small path they followed, but once they were halfway in, he asked, "Hey, can I show you guys something I found really quick?"

They agreed and followed him off the path and deeper into the wooded area, stepping over fallen trees and around the underbrush. When Matthew finally stopped, he pointed towards the tombstones.

"What is this, Matthew, a cemetery?" Agnes asked.

She approached the three headstones slowly while he explained. "There are these three headstones and nine small markers scattered about."

She moved closer to the headstone on the left. Running her fingers across their markings, she couldn't quite make them out. "They are too worn to read," she announced.

Colin approached her side. "Try this," he suggested, picking up a handful of moist dirt from the ground and wiping it across the engraving. The letters came into view, and Agnes read them aloud. "Colonel Twist," she announced, then she and Colin moved to the one in the middle. "Colonel Anderson," she added as they moved to the one on its right. And in conclusion, meet Colonel Irving."

The three of them stood at the foot of the graves, looking them over one by one.

"These would have to be Civil War colonels," Matthew announced.

She read the full names out loud once more: "Colonels Oliver Twist, Edward Clifford Anderson, and Washington Irving." She laughed. "Oliver Twist and Washington Irving? They weren't Confederate colonels." Glancing around, she saw no other headstones; there were only three. "Wait! It can't be. Oh my gosh, we've found it!" she exclaimed.

"Found what?" Matthew asked.

"I think we just found our funds to start Mystic Oysters." She kissed Matthew awkwardly with excitement. She then turned to Colin. "I've gotta go. Call me when you get back home. I love you."

"Where are you going?" Matthew called out as she began running back through the woods on the path they had just taken.

"I've got to call my brothers," she yelled over her shoulder. "You're gonna love this."

53

FREE

Gladys walked to the large picture window and looked down the narrow, stoned street. *I'm free,* she thought. *But can a person like me ever be completely free?* She waved her thoughts away. *I must stay busy, that's all,* she told herself and began to get dressed for the day. *I'll go into the town today and reacquaint myself with the city. I can grab lunch at that quaint café. I might even have a few glasses of wine. Why live in Italy if you can't appreciate the gifts of the land?*

Her walk into Siena was invigorating. Siena had checked all the marks of all the towns she had visited. Its charm alone was a sell, but the fact that the police were so laid-back gave her the ability to blend.

Sitting at an outside café table at Il Bandierina, she let her toes warm in the sun. Her eyes swept the Piazza del Campo as she listened to the many sounds bouncing off the large buildings. The waiter delivered her pizza and red wine, and she ate slowly, appreciating every bite of her first meal in her new city.

She agreed when the waiter asked if she'd like another glass of wine. But after he delivered her third glass, she was filled with an unrecognizable feeling: regret. *I can't go backward,* she told herself, and *I can't undo what's already been done.* The only person she needed to explain things to was Agnes. She asked the waiter for a pen and paper and began to write.

She thought of her first line in her head. "My life was taken from me the night I witnessed a triple murder." She paused before writing. Agnes knew the story. There was no need to try to explain what happened after. But for the first time in her life, she decided to admit the truth. She began writing.

Dear Agnes,

My life was taken from me the night I witnessed a triple murder. But, truth be known, I wasn't a good person even before that. I was an ungrateful child who only wanted to be out from under my parents' roof. God bless them; they were wonderful people. I also wanted things that didn't belong to me. To be more specific, Benjamin. I'm most sorry for losing Lottie's love, but I will never feel guilty. I wouldn't have had Henri, which was my greatest accomplishment in life.

I never loved Patrick, not romantically, at least. But we saved each other in a way. I helped him keep his business and gave him a child, and he gave Henri the father he deserved. When he and Maria died, I did the same for you. I gave you the family you deserved. I have no regrets about that. But now it's time for me to step out of the picture. You see, I stayed put until I knew you were happy and cared for. And once you turned down your ownership of our company, I knew it was time to go. That's when I began my exit.

I witnessed the murders on the yacht that night, and in retaliation, I stole a pile of jewels. They were blood money and just sitting there for the taking. I've gradually sold them off, one by one. But now was the time to sell them all so I could give Colin the company he deserved and Patrick the care he required. You will never see me again, but I leave knowing that you are part of a family and friends who love

you unconditionally, along with a man who would lay down his life for you. Always remember how much I love you,
   Gladys

She wiped her eyes and folded the paper. *When I return to the flat, I'll pull out the pages I printed from the Savannah archives and enclose them in this letter to Agnes. Then, she'll have the complete story and can do whatever she wishes with the information.* She shoved the letter into her purse and asked for the bill.

As she began her walk home, she crossed the piazza and turned onto the steep road toward her flat. She began to tire quickly from the upward slope and stopped to catch her breath. Looking up, she was standing under one of the many paintings of the Virgin Mary, enclosed for safekeeping. Several Italian cities showcased these for the locals to remember their faith. As she focused on this one, the words of the Memorare instantly popped into her mind. She hadn't thought of that prayer in fifty years, yet the words spilled out of her mouth,

"Remember, O most gracious Virgin Mary, that never was it known that anyone who fled to your protection, implored your help, or sought your intercession was left unaided." She didn't finish the prayer. Instead, she stopped and said, "I implore your help."

The answer popped into her mind. "Turn around." As she spun, she noticed she was standing in front of Chiesa di San Martino church. Fear gripped her. "Confession? I can't go to confession," she mumbled. A passerby gave her a strange look as she continued to try to reason with her conscience. But in the end, her heart pulled her across the street and into the church, where she could finally be completely free.

54

PROTECTORS

Agnes and her brothers were barely making headway. The tools Lottie had in the shed wouldn't get this job done. They needed more than two shovels and a post-hole digger. Darkness had set upon them quickly, and the thick woods blocked the moon's light. Agnes watched her breath take shape in the cold. *Pure adrenaline will keep them going all night,* she thought as she watched the flashlight beam begin to shake against the dirt.

After the sun went down, holding the two flashlights in place had been her one job. She laughed when her brothers positioned her, showing her where to send the light beams. Her arms ached after holding them in place for a few hours, so the minute the battery began to lose power on the first flashlight, she jumped at the chance to stop for the night.

"I think we need to call it a night," she announced. Her brothers seemed confused by her ability to walk away from treasure, so she softened the blow. "Let's take a break and get something to eat." That got their attention, and they quickly moved from the three-foot hole they had dug.

Once they had emptied the contents of her refrigerator, she

told them they were going home for the night. When they tried to argue, she put her foot down. "You can be back at sun-up, but you are all going home now. We need better shovels, so bring better equipment when you come back. They all agreed until she made her last command. "If we find treasure down there, we will call the police."

They began to argue that it was on her property, so it belonged to her, but she put up her hand. "I looked this up. The State will give you the object's monetary value if it's over one hundred years old. So, if it is gold, we will get paid. But we need to do this the right way." When they finally agreed, she added the most important part. "Just like Lottie told us, we will split everything."

The next few weeks were full of activity. As the legend had been told, they found gold buried under the colonel's headstone. There was so much gold that it took the City of Savannah's small excavators and lifts to bring it all to the surface.

Savannah was still in disbelief that the old story had been confirmed. Everyone wanted to get a glimpse of the piece of history being unearthed. Agnes allowed television crews and newspaper reporters to come and give reports to keep all the locals informed. Still, people began standing at the end of her driveway, trying to sneak their own peek. Most would come and go, but one lady in particular seemed different. She wasn't just gawking, hoping to glimpse real-life treasure. She seemed to be looking for something more.

Agnes had noticed her watching the dig site from the very beginning. She was old and used a cane, but there was something familiar about her face. Agnes had seen her somewhere before. Agnes had tried to approach her several times, but the lady would always leave the house and walk off along the bluff.

However, that day was different. Agnes had gone on a long walk. When she was almost home, she noticed the older lady standing at the end of her driveway. This time, Agnes approached her from behind. Agnes slowly moved in beside her. She propped her elbows on the white wood fence and peered into her yard. She felt the woman's stare, but Agnes didn't meet it.

The woman cleared her throat. In a soft voice, she said, "Good afternoon."

"Good afternoon," Agnes replied as she turned toward the woman's smiling face at the fence. *Wait. I know you,* Agnes thought. *But how? Kind eyes, a round face, and a small gap between her teeth. Where do I know you from?*

"Are you the young woman who owns the Mystic?" the woman asked.

Agnes thought about that description. Smiling at the woman, she admitted, "I've realized that no one can ever own the Mystic. I just live there." Agnes felt the woman's eyes reading her, but she didn't mind. *She's trying to decide whether to continue the conversation or end it,* Agnes thought.

"That's quite an answer from someone so young," the woman finally replied. She moved her cane into her left hand and reached out her right hand to introduce herself. "I'm Miss Annie. I didn't want to bother you before, but I just had to know."

"Know what?"

"About the slaves. I was always told that runaway slaves came through the Mystic; have you found any traces since you started diggin?"

"No. But I'm certain that slaves came through the land, too," Agnes answered.

Miss Annie raised her eyebrow, "Are you now?"

"Yes," Agnes answered without explaining further. Nodding toward the property, she asked, "Do you want to come see?"

Miss Annie looked down the driveway, then back to Agnes. Nodding slowly, she agreed. Agnes took the lead, and Miss Annie followed her. As they strolled down the driveway, Miss

Annie let her story unfold. "My mama told me this story, just like her mama told her. That's how we remember, you know? We tell our stories. She told me that an animal doctor lived on the Mystic. He had many horses; most of them had been in battles in the Civil War. They were undernourished and barely alive themselves. Still, they were able to carry wounded soldiers back to Savannah. But the sounds of those battles had messed those horses up good. They needed someone to comfort them once they got here. So, the old doctor took those horses in. You know, Lottie told me she still heard them sometimes."

"I'm sure she did," Agnes answered. Once again, she felt the older woman's eyes trying to read her before turning her attention back to the path.

Miss Annie picked up where she left off. "Well, that doctor was a good man who opposed slavery. So, he helped runaway slaves find freedom. People were already scared of his crazy horses, so they stayed clear of the land. It was the perfect place to build a hiding spot until he could take them by boat to Saint Helena Island at night."

Agnes listened intently. She could picture everything perfectly. She had heard their voices, and the story had now given them shape. Agnes replied, "I've only lived here a short time, but I've discovered so many interesting things on this land—things I couldn't put into place until now. Thank you, Miss Annie."

The older woman only nodded in response. But there was something in that nod—a tilt in her head or a look in her eye. Agnes was finally able to pinpoint where she knew her from. She could picture the black-and-white photograph of a much younger version of Miss Annie, sitting on the back steps of her house, drinking a bottled Coca-Cola with Lottie.

Agnes blurted out, "Oh my gosh, you are Annie. You and Lottie were friends. I have a picture of you in the house."

Miss Annie laughed, "Yes, ma'am. We sure were. When

Lottie and I were young, we realized we had much in common —we both had a connection to the past."

Agnes nodded. "It must have been a great comfort that you could confide in one another."

"Yes, it was," Miss Annie responded, then whispered, "and it still is."

They continued to walk until they came to the dig site. Miss Annie stopped a few feet away. She reached over and took Agnes' hand, then closed her eyes. Agnes did the same. All her senses came alive. She could hear the rustle of the leaves in the trees above and smell the mixture of the fresh soil that had been dug and the mud of the nearby marsh. Then she heard the distant singing. It started so low that she strained her ears to listen. But then it built to where Agnes could almost feel the breath of one of the many singers. She was surprised to hear Miss Annie begin to sing with them.

She wanted to open her eyes, but she was afraid the moment would be over if she did. So, she listened. It lasted only a moment, then the voices slowly faded.

Miss Annie's voice calling her name broke the silence, "Agnes?"

"Yes, ma'am?" she answered.

"The Mystic is safe in your hands. Take good care of them," she said.

Agnes nodded, acknowledging the weight of what Miss Annie had just said.

Leaning on her cane, Miss Annie turned to leave. She only took two steps before turning back to Agnes. "People like us can't change things. We definitely can't change the past. But we have to try really hard not to change the future. Lottie knew that, and you must understand that, too." Agnes let her words sink in and then nodded to Miss Annie, letting her know she understood. "I'll be seeing you again soon," she added and walked off in the direction they had come.

Agnes watched her depart but didn't follow. Something pulled her in the opposite direction. Her brain could no longer comprehend the longing in her heart, so she followed wherever it took her. She walked along the bay and past her house. Thoughts of Lottie flooded her mind with each step she took. All of her animosity melted away. She could feel Lottie's love. She now understood why Lottie hadn't told her everything and knew how hard it must have been for her.

She kept walking until she was standing at the point. Her eyes moved out to the Skidaway River, then scanned the bay and wetlands in every direction. Breathing in the cool salt air, she caught the slight scent of Chanel No. 5 and nodded in response. "Goodbye, Lottie," she whispered into the wind. "Rest in peace."

The sound of someone approaching brought her back to the present. Turning, she found Matthew staring at her. The sight of him tightened her stomach, and a grin began to form on her lips. Still, the worry on his face was concerning. "What's wrong?" she asked.

"I've seen this all before." He ran his hand across his face, deep in thought. "Remember how I told you I would see Lottie standing on this point, and when she would see me, her face would change to connect to the present. That's the same way you just looked."

Agnes smiled at him. "Yes, I remember you telling me that. But I'm definitely not Lottie." Although that was true, she realized how quickly her world had shifted. "Do you remember telling me that you thought she was watching and listening for something far away and how she would nod in response? Well, now I know."

"You know what?"

"I know that she wasn't listening to something far away; she was listening to those around her and nodding in response. She was their protection."

Agnes watched Matthew's face as he processed what she had just said. He looked out to the river and then back to her. "And who is their protection now?"

The loud sound of horses approaching made Matthew turn quickly toward the house. "What the hell is that?" he asked. Agnes laced her hand into his while his eyes searched for the source of the sound. He turned to her for answers.

"Remember all the tales you've heard about the Mystic? I think they might be true," Agnes whispered. "Let's go inside, and I'll fix you a glass of lemonade."

Shaking his head, he countered, "I think a shot of Whiskey might be more in order." He glanced back toward the river and remembered a conversation he and Agnes had a few weeks before, so he added. "Whatever this is, we'll figure it out together."

This time, Agnes added, "And it's sure gonna be fun figuring it out with you."

The End

ALSO BY LEIGH EBBERWEIN

The Saints of Savannah Series

The Blessing of the Celtic Curse

Just weeks before her wedding, Kathleen leaves behind her fiancé, Jack, on a six-week trip to Knock, County Mayo, Ireland. While Kathleen digs into the lives of her ancestors, she develops her own ties to Ireland. Her life, and that of the townsfolk of Knock, become intimately bound in unimaginable ways.

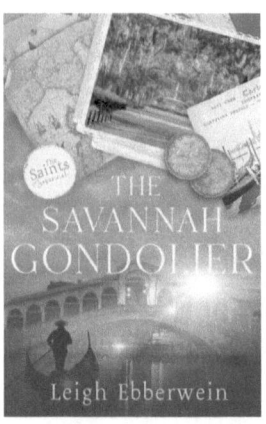

The Savannah Gondolier

When Maggie reunites with her childhood friend, Leo, she realizes he is running from his life in Venice, Italy. After offering him a job at her haunted adventure kayak company, Leo plans a new future for himself. However, he needs Maggie's help. She jumps at the chance to travel to his hometown of Venice and quickly understands that she is also running from her life in Savannah, or at least from her broken heart.

The Castle on Wassaw Sound

When Stephanie is offered a job, she had no idea it was for a renovation of a 250-YEAR-OLD castle that came with an irritating, kilt-wearing project manager. They quickly learn that they must work together to preserve this lost piece of Savannah's history. With time racing against them, a trip to Scotland may hold the key to their wild success—or whopping failure.

ACKNOWLEDGMENTS

I began researching this novel a few years ago after reading an article about oyster farmers on Prince Edward Island. The concept of Farm-to-Table from the ocean blew my mind, and I had to dig deeper. Several research files on my computer later, I began writing THE COTTAGE ON MYSTIC LANE. But all the research in the world can't replace experiencing somewhere firsthand, so last July, I began planning an October trip to Prince Edward Island.

Being a gal from the deep South, I never considered the weather in Canada. Still, I quickly discovered that tourism shuts down in the last week of August. I'm blessed to be married to a supportive husband who arranged to not only take me on a last-minute, whirlwind trip to Canada but also to eat dozens and dozens of oysters with me for research. You are truly the best!

God has also blessed me with many talented individuals who help me bring this novel to fruition. Thank you to my editor, Patrice MacArthur; my cover designer, Sarah Hansen, with Okay Creations; my fantastic marketing team at Cecilia Russo Marketing; and my wonderful Advance Readers, who helped me tie up all the loose ends.

Many books ago, I decided that Agnes' story would be about adoption. My family has been blessed by this beautiful, life-giving gift of love, and I want to share it with the world. I hope I was able to give you a glimpse through the eyes of Agnes' mom's character of Ruthie.

To all those who call me Mom (or Mayme), thank you for your unconditional love and support. My heart is full.

And finally, to my readers. I am so grateful for your love and support. Thank you for giving me the privilege to entertain you —if only for a little while.

EPILOGUE

Agnes hurried toward the house. There were so many things to be done before the big event, so she had woken up early not to miss her walk through the woods. There were nine horses who would wreak havoc on her if she didn't give them the attention they thought they deserved. All those sleepless nights wondering if she was losing her mind had been just an attention stunt. Once they had realized she could hear them, they demanded her acknowledgment.

The day they found the colonel's gold, she investigated the other nine markers and found the names of each animal. She stood beside each marker and called their name, and the horse would come to her. That is how she got to know each one of them. Each was a different size and had a different gait, but they were all stuck in this world together—in Savannah, on the Mystic.

But they weren't the only ones stuck. After Agnes' time with Miss Annie, she understood the people behind the hushed voices and occasional songs. Agnes still heard them, but unlike the horses, they didn't want or require her attention. She respectfully gave them distance. She knew they would find her if they needed her.

She couldn't fault any of them, of course. They had all been forgotten for so long. And in all reality, she needed them as much as they needed her. They brought her peace and kept her abilities focused. Still, she couldn't help but wonder what made them linger. Maybe it was the Mystic itself. Maybe the constant fog hovering somehow kept them trapped. She would never know. But she was thankful they had found each other.

Running back to the house, she quickly refocused her mind on the actual people in her life. It was a big day for them, and she could hardly wait to celebrate. She was thankful she didn't have to wait long.

Agnes recognized the scent in the air as the River Queen pulled alongside Fort Jackson's dock: oysters. The smell made sense because the whole night had been devoted to the wonderful mussels changing Savannah. It was almost unbelievable how far they'd come in only ten years.

Scanning the crowd, she searched for her family and friends. Everyone had responded they were coming except Matthew's parents. His father had called the night before to inform him that they could not come because his mom wasn't doing well. That was the only thing making the day not one hundred percent perfect.

Hundreds of people were trying to make their way into Old Fort Jackson. They moved with the flow, saying hello to familiar faces while excitedly waiting to walk through the large, teal-painted wooden doors. Once inside, the crowd went in different directions, following the cobblestone walkways.

The Fort was built to defend the city against enemy ships, and once again, it was being used to protect Savannah. Only this time, it was protecting the river itself. The waterfront land around Old Fort Jackson had become one of the main sites for the oyster filtration systems, with five smaller sites along the river. Month by month and year by year, the waters had become cleaner. Sea life had returned and the man-made reefs, set miles off the coast, were repopulating naturally. There couldn't be a better time to celebrate, and Old Fort Jackson was the perfect venue.

The first faces she recognized inside were those of the Oyster Stew Crew. They had a stand set up in the middle and were passing out cups of stew while some others were dancing to the music playing behind the stand. Agnes watched as they conversed with the many patrons who were eating happily. Lottie had known what she was doing when she turned the stew-making over to them.

Agnes spotted her friends standing alongside one of the white-washed brick walls and snuck over to say "hello." They watched her approach and held up their martini glasses to her.

"Are y'all already getting into trouble?" Agnes asked while investigating one of the glasses. "What are those?"

"We're only having one until after the presentation, then you can have one with us. They are dirty martini oyster shooters," Maggie replied.

Agnes shuttered, "Uh, no, thank you. Not now, not never." She went around the group, kissing each of her friends on the cheek. "I'm so happy you all could come; I know how hard it is to get away these days."

They congratulated her and offered her their love, then shooed her off. Agnes smiled as she walked away from them. *How did I ever get so lucky to have such good friends?* she thought. But she knew how. They each had to work to keep their friendship strong. The motto was true; "To have a friend, you must be a friend," and it was totally worth it with her tribe.

The announcer came over the intercom, calling for everyone's attention.

Matthew turned to Agnes, "Will you please hand me my speech cards from your purse?"

Agnes met his eyes, "Yes, but I added a few things."

He looked horrified. "I spent weeks working on that speech."

"I didn't change one thing you wrote; it's perfect. I only added pauses for dramatic effects."

"Whew. You scared me. Thank you," he whispered while taking the cards from her hand.

Everyone quieted as they called Matthew to the stage. He smiled at the crowd, then glanced down to his notes. His brow furrowed, but then he followed her suggestion.

Look to the Fort's turquoise doors.

Matthew looked to see his mom standing inside the doors. When he smiled, she waved high and proud. He stood tall, then began.

"For hundreds of years, the ocean took care of man, offering him the nourishment he needed to survive. Man responded by cherishing the waterways. Until one day, unfortunately, in the time we now live, man decided he was no longer responsible for protecting. Instead, he used the waterways for his own purposes. And the ocean responded."

Pause for the tug boat to spray water from their firefighting nozzles in a water salute.

The crowd cheered until the tug tooted its high-pitched whistle and moved down the channel. Matthew picked up where he left off. "Last year, the Savannah Oyster Project added over ten million juvenile oysters to the Savannah River. These oysters were brought in to filter the water and create habitats for other marine life, and we are seeing marvelous results.

He motioned for his family to come onto the stage. "We want our waters clean and a better tomorrow for our children. My family and I would like to thank you for supporting this project. Together, we can learn to cherish the waterways once again."

As the crowd cheered, Matthew hoisted their son, Benjamin, onto his hip. He gave Agnes a quick peck, then kissed the forehead of baby Charlotte, Lottie for short.

Agnes looked across the crowd at everybody who loved them so dearly, then back up to Matthew. Meeting her gaze, he pulled her in closer and leaned over once again for a soft, longer kiss. She recognized the look on his face; she had seen it several times before when he was extremely happy and proud. She had seen it on their wedding day, the day they broke ground at Mystic Oyster Company, and the birth of both their children. But today, it had one added element that reminded her of another time.

She could picture it like it was yesterday. The snow falling at the Grotto at Notre Dame. She had been so distressed and contemplated leaving school. He had been there for her that night and had kissed her before they parted. He wore that exact expression when he had pulled back from their kiss. They both had felt the shift in the universe, but this time, she could identify it. It's the feeling of knowing your destiny.

STOP BY FOR A VISIT

If you love the beauty of Savannah and enjoy traveling the world through a novel, visit Leighebberwein.com. There, you'll find questions for your Book Club, live video scenes, up-to-date information on future books, and so much more!

        facebook.com/Lebberwein
        instagram.com/lebberwein
        tiktok.com/@lebberwein

www.ingramcontent.com/pod-product-compliance
Lightning Source LLC
Chambersburg PA
CBHW060553080526
44585CB00013B/550